INTO
THE
VACUUM

Christian Mission and Modern Culture

EDITED BY
ALAN NEELY, H. WAYNE PIPKIN,
AND WILBERT R. SHENK

In the Series:

INTO
THE
VACUUM

Being the Church in an
Age of Barbarism

GORDON SCOVILLE

TRINITY PRESS
INTERNATIONAL
HARRISBURG, PENNSYLVANIA

First published by
TRINITY PRESS INTERNATIONAL
P.O. Box 1321
Harrisburg, PA 17112

Trinity Press International is a division
of the Morehouse Group.

Scripture quotations are from the New Revised Standard
Version Bible, copyright 1989, Division of Christian Education
of the National Council of the Churches of Christ in the United
States of America, and are used by permission.

Cover design: Brian Preuss

Library of Congress Cataloging-in-Publication Data
Scoville, Gordon.
    Into the vacuum, being the church in an age of barbarism /
Gordon Scoville.
        p. cm. — (Christian mission and modern culture)
    Includes bibliographical references.
    ISBN 1–56338–238–5
        1. Mission of the church.   2. Church and the world.
    3. Christianity and culture—United States—History—19th
    century.   4. Christianity and culture—United States—
    History—20th century.   5. United States—Civilization—
    19th century. 6. United States—Civilization—20th century.
    I. Title.   II. Series.
    BV601.8.S37   1998
    277.3'0829—dc21
                                                    97–32869
                                                    CIP

Printed in the United States of America

98 99 00 01 02 03   6 5 4 3 2 1

Contents

96385

"Every plant that my heavenly Father has not planted will be uprooted."

—*Matthew 15:13*

Preface to the Series

Both Christian mission and modern culture, widely regarded as antagonists, are in crisis. The emergence of the modern mission movement in the early nineteenth century cannot be understood apart from the rise of technocratic society. Now, at the end of the twentieth century, both modern culture and Christian mission face an uncertain future.

One of the developments integral to modernity was the way the role of religion in culture was redefined. Whereas religion had played an authoritative role in the culture of Christendom, modern culture was highly critical of religion and increasingly secular in its assumptions. A sustained effort was made to banish religion to the backwaters of modern culture.

The decade of the 1980s witnessed further momentous developments on the geopolitical front with the collapse of communism. In the aftermath of the breakup of the system of power blocs that dominated international relations for a generation, it is clear that religion has survived even if its institutionalization has undergone deep change and its future forms are unclear. Secularism continues to oppose religion, while technology has emerged as a major source of power and authority in modern culture. Both confront Christian faith with fundamental questions.

The purpose of this series is to probe these developments from a variety of angles with a view to helping the church understand its missional responsibility to a culture in crisis. One important resource is the church's experience of two centuries of cross-cultural mission that has reshaped the church into a global Christian *ecumene*. The focus of our inquiry will be the church in modern culture. The series (1) examines modern/postmodern culture from a missional point of view; (2) develops the theological agenda that the church in modern culture must address in order to recover its own integrity; and (3) tests fresh conceptualizations of the nature and mission of the church as it engages modern culture. In other words, these volumes are intended to be a forum where conventional assumptions can be challenged and alternative formulations explored.

This series is a project authorized by the Institute of Mennonite Studies, research agency of the Associated Mennonite Biblical Seminary, and supported by a generous grant from the Pew Charitable Trusts.

Editorial Committee

ALAN NEELY
H. WAYNE PIPKIN
WILBERT R. SHENK

Acknowledgments

For their encouragement, support, and/or critique I want to thank Wilbert R. Shenk, Gayle Gerber Koontz, Henry J. Dyck, Ted Koontz, Jacob W. Elias, William Smith, James M. Lapp, Diane Lodge-Peters, Marvin Shaw, Mike Gard, and others too numerous to mention here. For their friendship in the crucial beginning stages of this volume: Dee Mobley and Glover and Mary Wagner. For daily manifestation of God's grace not only while I struggled to write but also while I wrestled to minister: Marie Scoville, rancher, artist, and wife. None of the aforementioned bear responsibility for what I have written.

Introduction

The inception of this volume probably occurred in the summer of 1993. At that time I served as the pastor of a "mainline" Protestant congregation[1] well along in a process of numerical decrease and internal decay. Convinced that the principal reason for its deterioration arose from a common perception of this church as "not standing for anything," and hence sure that decline resulted from an inability to offer a purpose for participation in congregational functions, I found myself confronting one of the congregation's lay leaders regarding the importance of constitutional identity. The church's constitution had long since drifted into a condition of disrepair. "How can people be expected to involve themselves in church activity if there is no governing declaration of mission identifying why they should get active here?" I asked the leader. "Why should people get involved if they don't know what the established criteria of involvement are?" I continued. "How can we expect people to care about what we're doing if we have neither constitutional means of saying that Christian life is important nor any stated expectations concerning how we believe it must be lived?" I thought my questions pointed clearly to the obvious fallacy in the way the congregation functioned. But the leader recoiled from the overtones of exclusivism in my objections and responded passionately that "I, for one, do not want to be in the position of unfairly laying down rules and excluding the people who never come to church!"

During ensuing days I became increasingly frustrated and angered over this impassioned rebuttal and over other similar refutations in the parish. I thought, "If we have to include those 'who *never* come,' then we can place *no* definable limits on who we are or on what we do. After all, someone who never comes could object to whatever limit we might establish." Discussion of the matter with my wife provoked her lucid observation, "Who wants to belong to a church that anyone can belong to? If membership is not special, then why be a member?" I felt anger not only at the absurdity of tolerance affirmed *ad nauseam* but at the futility of trying to alter the affirmation and its concomitant organizational decay. Moreover, I recollected earlier occasions in my pastorate, experiences of losing faith that a "program fix" could rectify the situation, of seeking to improve attendance by being entertaining on Sunday morning, and of beginning to feel tired and hollow inside.

When I examined my experience, my mind ran increasingly to the metaphor of a black hole. The church paralleled an exhausted star whose ongoing collapse exerted a gravitational pull sucking energy and life into nothingness. Consistent with astronomical theory, the hole remained largely invisible. The congregation continued to operate normally, going through the motions of worship, staffing offices, and the like. But the hole became visible in its effects on nearby matter: manifest boredom and apathy among congregants and visitors, and steady corrosion of the body through declining income and participant burnout.

I mentioned my metaphorical rumination to my wife, and she replied, "Oh, of course, a vacuum." Indeed. In this pastoral assignment, I had stepped into something of a vortex or whirlpool suction into a process whose gravitational force required the spiritual emptiness that prospers amid disintegration into the limitless nether region of "not standing for anything" and not "excluding the people who never come."

And so this volume started. Being enough of a meta-physical wholist or *gestaltist* to figure that my parish could not act as it did without the organic support of a greater whole given to like operation, I intuited that the congregation must be a microfeature of a larger tapestry. In support of this intuition I recalled Paul's adaptation of the ancient image of the body and its various parts. Christian community possessed an organic unity analogous to that of Roman and Greek conceptions of a cohesive political organism. Paul reasoned that no part of the church could undergo an experience without all other Christians being in some manner similarly affected.[2] Hence, "If one member suffers, all suffer together with it" (1 Cor. 12:26a). Paul's ecclesial ontology now captured my attention in a sense more personal than ever before: Within the universal body I was the pastor of a "member" congregation that clearly suffered continuing descent into a vacuum. I wondered both how wide into ecclesiastical circles this fall reached and in what sociohistorical likenesses it could be perceived.

The seventeenth- and eighteenth-century Enlightenment overthrew the traditional authority of moral claims grounded in Christian and Aristotelian teleology.[3] Instead of basing morality on action either to obey divine will or to realize the potential of essential human nature, the Enlightenment proffered the capacity of autonomous reason to anchor conduct in supratraditional or "objective" standards of judgment. Immanuel Kant, for example, proposed principles that everyone could embrace regardless of historical relativity. The rational test for such maxims was simple enough: Can you will with consistency that all people should at all times obey your principle? It followed, then, that Kant might authorize that humans always be treated as ends and never as means. But without teleological motive (i.e., without the possibility of uniting a present act with its true purpose), neither he nor any other

Enlightenment philosopher could explain why such authorization ought to be obeyed.

So it came to be that this sort of failure to ground moral practice impelled Enlightenment thought to construct something of a bipolar world where reason concerned itself at once with a public domain given to mathematical certainties of "fact," while cordoning off a private realm of "values" given over to the unverifiable and subjective assertions of religion and morality. The state, now a kind of surrogate for God as the agent of social cohesion, gradually extended the bureaucratic organization whose scientific technology promised the only remaining effective means of public order and control amid the multiplication of competing values arising from sundry private worldviews. Indeed, the ascendant "pluralism" of these clashing *Weltanschauungen* produced both enough fragmentation of shared purpose and sufficient disintegration of collective identity to warrant massive state intervention to rein in the momentum toward chaos. Severed from moral restraint, the marketplace itself became an unregulated turmoil of atoms, individualists badly in need of public control lest private competition become unfettered social disarray.

Individuals and groups proclaimed their "rights," but in a world without a common rationality these easily became an arbitrary assertion of power that ironically excused bureaucratic repression of individual freedom in the name of necessary order. For its part, however, managerial bureaucracy esteemed an efficient control that was as much illusion as reality in a universe where natural and human processes resist total predictability. But rhetoric about efficiency-cum-effectiveness dramatized a salutary response to social needs, thereby legitimizing managerial desire for increased power.

Beneath both individualist self-assertion and bureaucratic regimentation, then, was a common "will to power" that vindicated Friedrich Nietzsche's observation that

Enlightenment rationalizations concealed an entirely non-rational reliance upon the arbitrary decisions of the will. Modern aspirations, whatever they consciously or ideologically declare, land perforce in an ethical vacuum where power in principle knows no restraint. Contending factions *must* fight to prevail (or, short of victory, struggle until they are exhausted). Alasdair MacIntyre alludes to the battles of contesting positions and says "that the moral resources of the [modern] culture allow us no way of settling them rationally.... It follows that our society cannot hope to achieve moral consensus." He continues by observing that post-Enlightenment critics see through the "falsifying masquerades" of diverse systems of belief, and hence with thorough skepticism apprehend that "beliefs, allegiances to conceptions of justice, and the use of particular modes of reasoning about action will appear... as disguises assumed by arbitrary will to further its projects, to empower itself" (MacIntyre 1984:252; 1988:395, 396).

Again, it ensues from the collapse of Enlightenment hopes that the core of our civilization would likely be imploding into a moral vacuum. I hypothesize both that this is the case and that my experience as a pastor occasioned encounter with particular social groups who manifested their own variety of witness to what happens once caught in the radius of the central implosion. In any event, there is urgency in hearing that our society in principle is bereft of restraint on capricious exercise of power. The precise term for the condition that unfolds from the disintegration of such constraint is barbarism. MacIntyre developed the hypothesis that I am attempting not only to echo but to buttress. He discerns that "the barbarians are not waiting beyond the frontiers; they have already been governing us for quite some time" (MacIntyre 1984:263). Unchecked power—now egoistic, now authoritarian—thrives in the vacuum.

I do not know when precisely this age of barbarism began; only that it seems always to have been the dark underside of the boisterous proclamations of progressive "enlightenment." Somewhere, sometime it was as if we crossed a line and thereafter could do nothing but march from one holocaust to another, each with its own scale and expression of destruction. I think of Walter Wink's somewhat parallel concern to focus on and interpret the Bible's idea of "Principalities and Powers." These have a simultaneous reality as invisible spirit and visible institutional manifestation of that spirituality. Institutions intended to accomplish good get twisted by a corrupting descent into reliance upon "domination" for order. The Powers become malignant, violence becomes the prevailing stuff of social exchange, and somewhere people pass beyond the brink into unleashed brutality (see Wink 1992:Intro., Pt. 1, esp. pp. 3, 40). Wink sees this process at work in the United States, as, among other things, many Americans rush to view films—*The Texas Chain Saw Massacre, The Evil Dead,* and others—that depict "the assault of pure evil" while perhaps signifying a nation "in which violence has become the ultimate concern, an elixir, sheer titillation, an addictive high, a substitute for relationships"(Wink 1992:24, 25). If this and hypotheses of barbarism are true, then, with MacIntyre, we grasp that "we are all already in a state so disastrous that there are no large remedies for it"(MacIntyre 1984:5).

Prescription for being the authentic church follows both from analysis of the historical context in which we live and from the *telos* toward which God calls us. For, unlike the skepticism in the ideation and social practice characteristic of post-Enlightenment culture, Christians do have a *telos,* a purposeful aim to be signs in history of the in-breaking reign of God that manifested itself through the suffering love of Jesus Christ, a love that (so our faith confesses) will prevail in the end.[4] On the one hand, then, we find our authenticity by worshiping the God revealed in

Jesus. Stated otherwise, in the words of the Shorter Catechism authored by the Westminster Assembly of 1643–1653, "Man's chief end is to glorify God" (quoted in Brauer 1971:862). On the other hand, we recognize the inauthenticity, the cost of fusing with a cultural regime that busies itself with collapsing into a moral vacuum—the disintegration of our identity as Christians.

So I underscore the importance of *being* the church, existing integrally as a community capable of self-identification as Christian. *Being* is that which resists nonbeing, opposes the void, recoils from the vacuum. Against death, disease, modern meaninglessness, and other threats of nonbeing, we can appropriate the wisdom in Paul Tillich's affirmation of "the courage to be" in spite of these menaces. The church, as Tillich suggested, has ontological ground in God for courageous refusal of the vacuity of modernity. Tillich also emphasized that Christian life participates in the dialectical movement of "separation" and "reunion," of "no" and "yes" that characterizes existence. In our contemporary historical context, therefore, the church can acknowledge that its "yes" to the predominant cultural order brings it—as a participant!—into something corrupting and deeply degenerative. The dialectical turn of time now summons our oppositional "no" to culture in order to say "yes" to Christian identity, and thereupon to declare a new "yes" to culture by offering it the gift of an authentic witness to Christ.[5]

In the Johannine writings Jesus declares, "My kingdom is not from this world" (John 18:36a). Indeed, Jesus' followers similarly "do not belong to the world" that hates them as it "hated" their Lord (17:14). John means the world as human sociopolitical power shapes it to deceive, not as God created it to live (cf. 1:10; 3:17; 12:47).

John sees that notwithstanding God's good intention to love human civilization by sending the Son into it, the absolute newness of Christ's life jolts societal order that wants self-deceptively to function as if institutional ruts constitute truthfulness. The disciples living in Jesus' name deliver a similar jolt; so the breach between the church that knows Christ and the faithless unknowing of established society and authority is sharp enough (15:18–16:4a), and in the New Testament shared widely enough (cf. Matt. 20:25–28; Mark 10:42–45; Luke 22:24–27; Rom. 12:2; 1 Cor. 5:12–13; 6:1–2; Gal. 1:4; Eph. 2:15; 4:17–24; Phil. 2:14–15; 1 Pet. 2:4–10; et al.), that Gerhard Lohfink speaks of Jesus as the initiator of a "contrast-society" whose distinctive identity is such as to mark "a line which admits of no blurred borders" between the church and the surrounding social environment (Lohfink 1982:128, see also 56, 95, 116–117, 122–127, 129–132).

The prescribed church is in fundamental terms the opponent of post-Enlightenment culture. This culture worships in the "pluralist" pantheon; the church follows Christ to the Trinity. The contrast, as we will observe below, continues: unleashed power versus cruciform nonsuperiority; calculating technical reason versus the surprise of the Holy Spirit; one-dimensional bondage to life without *telos* versus eschatological hope for God's reign; slipshod privatization of "values" versus disciplined communal covenant; and the large-scale "solutions" of abstract, impersonal bureaucratization versus the small-scale possibilities of concrete, flesh-and-blood personalization. ("We are all already in a state so disastrous that there are no large remedies for it.") In a word, these church-culture distinctions are of such elemental significance that we should all pray for the courage to be people whose proper domain "is not from this world."

A "mainline" Protestant periodical recently issued a candid account of the deterioration of its denomination. Noting precipitous membership decline since the early 1970s, "evangelistic anemia" that fails to address "today's pluralistic environment," lack of "a *distinctive* Christian norm" to counter the attractions of other volunteer organizations, and signs of being "increasingly a geriatric church," the article concluded with reference to what seemed to be "a more fundamental problem" with the denomination's operation: "I rarely have the feeling in our gatherings that we are gripped by a higher power. I do not often see fire in our eyes. Dare I say this? Much of the time we are boring" (Allen 1994:16, 17).

My thesis is that experiences of boredom and apathy are symptoms of a deeper disintegration of ecclesial *raison d'être* (read: loss of the worship of God) as church practices allow capture within the vortex of a post-Enlightenment culture whose logic—without shared *telos* there is no rational way to resolve moral disputes, so no restraint in principle on arbitrary will to power, so no final defense against violence—is well advanced in collapsing into a vacuum devoid of the capacity to form consensus regarding what is right. Ecclesial complicity in this cultural incapacity produces churches where vitality drains away into the ennui whose spread is commensurate with failure to trust and to embody Christian identity. Here and there the epitaph of local congregations might read, "They did not stand for anything." Death follows from our refusal to distinguish ourselves from a culture that mutates from tolerance to nihilism, from positive thinking to solipsism, from idealism to cynicism. Instead of choosing Christian distinction, we become "liberals" and "conservatives" who exhaust ourselves in crusades that feel righteous in proportion to our success at veiling the will to power at the root of political campaigns. Instead of choosing obedience to the cruciform humility of our Lord, we rush to mega-size through "Church Growth" techniques and other ways of exalting market-driven technology.

What else in the culture is left to exalt? Our mega-expectations fail to stake out a difference from the bureaucratization whose scale increases and whose control tightens.

What else can maintain social order? Lacking the integrity of our distinct being, we cannot be surprised to hear reports that "we are boring." This is my thesis: that we stepped into a process that involves disintegrating into a moral vacuum from which the only exit is to become the church of committed disciples.

In succeeding sections of this volume I attempt to ground my argument in a variety of experiential, historical, and theological materials. I offer, first, some personal glimpses of pastoral ministry in the vacuum. Second, I present examples largely from nineteenth- and twentieth-century American history that demonstrate a comprehensive process in which bureaucracy feeds symbiotically on cultural disintegration while advancing into barbarism. Next, I attempt to exemplify the vacuum both in the ongoing development of "mainline" Protestant "decline" and in my pastoral experience amid this deterioration.[6] Fourth, I point to seeds of comparable disintegration among "evangelical" churches, although, in their case, numerical prosperity masks a serious condition of decadence.[7] Last, I suggest prescriptions regarding what the post-Enlightenment church must do to get right. These directions finish by referring to practical possibilities that tentatively mark the kind of starters that ecclesiology will need to develop.

I write from my pastoral experience and both for pastors-cum-church persons who are unafraid to examine frankly the sociohistorical conditions now shaping ministry, and for academic theologians who are not afraid to hear from the front-line just how grim the situation is. Methodologically, I embrace a back-and-forth interplay or dialogue between personal experience, historical observation, and conceptual analysis. The British historian E. P. Thompson carried out this reciprocal method by employing "the disciplined historical discourse of the proof," consisting "in a dialogue between concept and evidence, a dialogue conducted by successive hypotheses, on the one hand, and empirical research on the other" (Thompson 1978:39, see also 41–42). Investigators repeatedly set up interaction between concepts or hypotheses as provisional explanations on the one hand, and evidence drawn from actual ideas and events of history on the other, until the two approach synthesis in the final composition. In what follows in this volume, I leave to the reader to judge whether my conceptual hypotheses—vacuum, barbarism, and the like—bring light to the real experiential and historical evidence.

Most important, perhaps, I wanted to write this volume because I am concerned that too many pastors and ecclesiastical officials have a vested stake in remaining unconscious of the historical vortex that can swallow us into something that bodes a very ugly future. Evangelism in America, in other words, will be harder than most of us ever imagined, for the reason that we ourselves are so largely captured by a status quo that depends for its existence on the destruction of things such as Christian mission.

1

Vignettes from the Vacuum
Pastoral Ministry amid the Collapse of Church Identity

During preparation for Pentecost Sunday the church organist confronts me: "Pastor, Memorial Day weekend is coming up. Why can't we sing patriotic hymns?"

✹✹✹

For months I work closely with a neighboring pastor. Our respective churches have a long-standing practice of ecumenical cooperation. One day my colleague resorts to cynicism. "Wonderful. Pentecost and the Spirit approach," he drones sarcastically. "Three cheers for the church. Then let's disband for summer vacation."

✹✹✹

On Easter Sunday the assembled worshipers barely fill half the available seating space. After the service one of the congregation's old-timers reflects, "We used to be the only show in town. But now it's hard to compete with the basketball game on TV."

✹✹✹

A deaconess motions me to the side of the meeting room. She expresses confusion: "Sometimes people ask what our church stands for. I don't know how to answer them."

Early on a Friday morning the treasurer, a prominent member of a powerful family within the congregation, comes to my office to propose imminent baptisms for several of her kin. "I don't know how you feel about it," she queries, "but we would like the baptisms to be a special family moment. Do they have to be a part of Sunday service?"

***

Church members gather for the day's activity. The assembly is considerably larger than the congregation's usual extra worship gatherings. What is on the agenda for this particular occasion? Cleaning the building and grounds.

***

On Wednesday I ask the youth group about their experience in church. Their response is resounding and unanimous: "Boring!" The following Sunday I listen to the sound of just my voice and that of the choir, and I notice that the moderator is sleeping.

***

By the sixth month of service in the parish, I am aware that certain buzzwords and phrases saturate the speech of church members—like "staying busy," or "keeping busy," or "so busy." I wonder what these declarations mean. All sections of the congregation speak this way, whether they be working or retired, parents or single, women or men, students or employed, well-to-do or not. Among the thoughts that occur to me, the one borne out most in observation is this: The church exists on a flat date-book surface right next to the appointed demands of the sewing circle, the Lions Club, the basketball team, and the like. These associations and the church are experienced as equivalent drains on time.

The congregation assembles for meeting. The topic is "how to increase participation in church functions." People repeatedly assert: "The school system tries to monopolize so much time. They used to make Monday 'church day' and held no extracurricular activities on that day. They encouraged kids to take Monday and participate in church. Now, though, the school wants all the time."

Collapse of Church Identity

When the church organist wanted to sing patriotic hymns, she wanted to do that and more; she wanted to reassure herself and the civic community that the church *believed what the community believed.*[1] She wanted to dissolve the distinction between the two. This conflation is the central fact of the context that gave rise to all the events cited above.

Recapitulate the experiences: a large turnout clean the building and grounds in order to preserve the *community's* chapel; a deaconess expresses confusion about *church* identity because it has none apart from the community; the treasurer seeks family-oriented baptisms outside of Sunday worship because, unlike the church, the family makes a *distinctive* claim on her life; and the church forms part of a monochrome pursuit of busyness because, like other clubs and associations, it exists as a *community* function. Here the mission of the church is to serve the community *on the community's terms.*

The vignettes also disclose experiential consequences of church-community conflation: pastoral cynicism results when the secular calendar replaces the church's birthday with the onset of summer vacation; a parishioner offers wistful resignation as his response to cultural attractions of television that compete with and shrink worship participation; church members grumble over the public school's assumption that it can take from the church without giving back; and boredom settles in as Christians find themselves unable to hear in worship something that they could not hear somewhere else. (Can anything be heard in Christian assembly if nothing distinctive is happening there? Is boredom avoidable if there is only the domestication in which everybody anticipates that everyone else will invoke a "nice day"? That is, can there be vitality if there is no permission for God to surprise us?[2])

Again, in sum, the church tries to serve the community by merging with the language and culture of the latter. But the merger turns out to be troubled, for the community conveys influences that undermine the church. There is no defense against these powers when, as in my experience, the congregation's Christian identity has already collapsed or dissolved into the surrounding culture. If the pastor seeks to restore some identifiable Christian course that could counter the implosion into nothingness, it soon becomes necessary to propose some disciplined constraint on church-as-catering-service-to-the-community. But such a proposal immediately encounters the objections of congregational leaders that the church should be friendly and caring and not be an authority that hampers the sharing of good-natured fellowship. Any establishment of disciplinary limits might offend someone.

Although in some circles it has become something of a knee-jerk defense mechanism to associate his name with sectarian excess, Stanley Hauerwas has a grasp of the dynamics being discussed here. He writes that ministerial "authority is now primarily constituted by... ability to deliver pastoral services" to those in traumatic distress and not by capacity for "liturgical leadership and the moral formation" of the congregants. He sees that pastors exercise "compassionate care" because consumers are searching for churches able to satisfy emotional longings. The customers want "a life-style enclave" that shares good feelings; formation to embody "Christian convictions" is quite another matter. Hauerwas realizes that ministers, unless they become practitioners of a kind of contemporary heresy, must incline to

offer unconditional acceptance of others in a society where
"we seek to be understood and to understand—not to be
judged" (Hauerwas 1991:95, 96; see also 16, 93–94, 98).

The issue, of course, is *not* caring versus discipline. No
pastor should enter ministry without aspiring to love people, to love life. The question is: What does it mean to be
loving in a world productive of disintegration? Part of the
answer is certainly that congregations do not integrate, do
not cohere, without the collective demonstration of moral
courage. Such bravery, in turn, is the fruit of disciplined
development in the faith. We must examine the prejudg-
ments that accompany the words *discipline* (Does it equal
authoritarianism?) and *care* (Does it mean limitless,
unconditional *catering?*). Without clarity respecting the
moral requirements of Christian communion, we are ill-
prepared to respond to the history now engulfing us in the
reality that morality is over.

2

The Symbiosis of Bureaucracy and Cultural Disintegration:
Entering an Age of Barbarism

Marketplace Chaos, Agrarian Populism, and the End of American Morality in 1896

If in the complex totality of social ideation and practice that constituted nineteenth-century American culture there was any belief that approached universal consensus, confidence in individual freedom was certainly that conviction (see Bellah 1992:xix). A spokesman for the antebellum Republican Party declared that industrializing America would advance manufacturing and commerce as "missionaries of freedom."[1] This liberty expressed itself in the widespread aspiration to become independent entrepreneurs and landed farmers. The fee-simple, 160-acre provisions of the Homestead Act of 1862 ratified the desire for wide diffusion of property so that people could pursue lives as independent yeomen. Independence, however, coupled with Protestant affirmations of individual responsibility and "character" as expressed in the virtues of industry, perseverance, frugality, thrift, sobriety, punctuality, honesty, and initiative.[2]

Americans buttressed individual freedom by relying on John Locke's principle of limiting the power of government while granting space for the free interaction of individuals in a state of nature. Locke made the modifying point that a liberal society, divorced from feudal ties, needed government as the last outpost of legitimate coercion. Americans, however, directed their attention to the westward frontier, surely a natural setting for the exercise of Lockian freedom, and wondered what possible need there could be for government interference in private affairs.[3]

Prior to the Civil War, much in the nation seemed to work to further the ideal of the free individual. A proprietary economy prospered on a small scale favorable to individualism. Individuals or small partnerships commonly owned manufacturing establishments. Northern firms hired an average of ten workers. Landowning farmers in the North were double the number of tenants and farm laborers. After the War opportunity still abounded for, in Daniel Boorstin's apt phrase, "the Go-Getters," those who discovered, invented, or otherwise profited amid the material development of the continent.[4] Individual freedom was a plausible belief on a landscape where railroad tracks were freshly laid, land was newly settled, and factories were initially built.[5]

Indeed, as observed by Robert N. Bellah, in a nation that drew simultaneously on the heritage of New England Puritanism for biblical images of covenantal or collective responsibility for the social order, and on the legacy of Rome-to-Montesquieu-classicism for republican ideas of virtuous self-renunciation for the good of the republic, by the nineteenth century Americans increasingly trumped these traditions with self-interested liberal utilitarianism. This liberalism focused on *my* happiness-*cum*-freedom and eventually overmatched any kind of self-denial by dramatizing the obvious "success" that followed from unhindered pursuit of the marketplace's main chance.[6]

The economic environment for this quest began radically to change. Industrialization accelerated, and following 1867, excepting depression years, more than two thousand miles

of railroad track advanced annually. Paired with achievements in telegraphy (and later with the telephone), the
conduct of business accelerated and broadened. An exten-
sive national market began to take shape. Factories
expanded to accommodate increased sales. The Baldwin
locomotive works exemplified the expansion as it grew
from six hundred workers in the mid-1850s to three thousand two decades later.[7]

Certain of the "Go-Getters" in business rose to the top of
the competitive scramble in the American market and struggled for the power to stay at the pinnacle. Earlier in the century, state legislatures established "general incorporation
laws." For a nominal cost of registration and a willingness to
comply with easy rules, these laws allowed businessmen
rapidly to expedite the formation of corporations. By the
1870s and 1880s, experiments in "vertical" and "horizontal
integration" enlarged the scope of corporate activity. The
former obtained control backward to the source of raw materials and forward through distribution of finished products.
The latter set prices in a particular industry, first, through
informal cartels and, later, through trusts and holding companies—the last denoted the formation of corporations into
larger corporations, a practice without sanction under the
earlier general incorporation laws. Effected essentially to sta-
bilize prices and restrain "ruinous" competition, these
experiments met with varying degrees of success.[8]

Small-scale competitors apprehended them as a threat
to the freedom implied in the ideal of "each man his own
boss" (see Porter 1973:43–71, 89–90). For example, travel-
ing salesmen increasingly found themselves transformed
into employees of corporations integrating into marketing.
In later observations, P. E. Dowe, a representative of one of
the travelers' associations, worried that "trusts have come…
as a curse for this generation and a barrier to individual
enterprise. What will be the prospects for our children? God-
Almighty alone knows."[9] Israel Washburn, a prominent

antebellum Republican from Maine, had already expressed the fear "that the money-power will be too much centralized—that the lands and property of the country, in the course of time may come to be held or controlled by a comparatively small number of people" (quoted in Foner 1970:22).

Even as corporations threatened individual freedom, they also appeared to undermine character. Honesty, for example, confronted what Chicago journalist Henry Demarest Lloyd noted in 1881: "The Standard [Oil Company] has done everything with the Pennsylvania legislature, except refine it" (quoted in Ginger 1965:32). In point of fact, Standard Oil's reported use of bribery to get Pennsylvania legislators to secure its effective monopoly over that state's pipelines was only a salient instance of widespread corporate practice. The Sherman Antitrust Act of 1890 represented an attempt to defeat such corruption and to preserve proprietary opportunity, but in the name of another menace to freedom—stronger regulation by national government.[10]

If in 1890 Americans could have called a halt to the frenetic pace of their politico-economic struggle, they might have recollected cautionary words like those rendered in 1774 by Nathaniel Niles, the noted Calvinist and devotee of Jonathan Edwards. Concerned about the implications of individualistic self-assertion, Niles lamented that when a person's "affection is turned on private interest, he will become regardless of the common good, and when he is detached from the community in heart, his services will be very precarious at best, and those will not be expected at all which imply self-denial" (quoted in Bellah 1992:30–31). Bellah comments on Niles: "He correctly pointed out that the utilitarian conception of society... would inevitably collapse into chaos" (Bellah 1992:30).

As it was, Americans plunged ahead into the competitive turmoil of the marketplace. Corporate "integration" offered to cohere society, but on behalf of yet another—albeit bureaucratized—private interest. The American version of Thomas Hobbes's jangle of clashing interests continued until it reached its logical conclusion—the depression of 1893. Markets could not consume at the level necessary for profit. As a result, 642 banks and sixteen thousand other businesses failed. Out of a workforce of fifteen million, three million lost their jobs. Farm prices sank to new lows in a thirty-year pattern of decline. Wheat dropped from $2.06 per bushel in 1866 to $.95 in 1874 to $.49 in 1894; corn declined from $.66 in 1866 to $.31 in 1878 to $.21 in 1896.[11]

Evidence of disintegration was all about. Workers, for example, confronted and fought against the sinking incomes and the unsafe working conditions that characterized depression. In 1893, regarding lack of safety in particular, one of every ten railroad employee operators was injured, and one of every 115 died on the job. Annually, throughout the decade, Pennsylvania miners suffered one injury for every 150 workers. Labor strikes involved 129,521 participants in 1881 and 499,489 in 1886. By 1894 an unparalleled 750,000 laborers refused to work. Two uprisings especially exemplified the tumult of the 1890s. In 1892 at Homestead, Pennsylvania, strikers engaged in armed struggle with Pinkertons hired by the Carnegie Steel Company. And in 1894, led by Eugene V. Debs's American Railway Union, a strike against the Pullman Palace Car Company at Pullman, Illinois, quickly spread across the nation as other workers joined in a boycott of railroads using Pullman cars. By midsummer of that year, thousands of tons of freight ceased to move.[12] To the *New York Times,* the boycott featured "the greatest battle between labor and capital that has ever been inaugurated in the United States" (quoted in Brecher 1972:82).

During the Pullman boycott, President Grover Cleveland's Attorney General, Richard Olney, offered his interpretation of the new contingencies: "We have been brought to the ragged edge of anarchy and it is time to see whether the law is sufficiently strong to prevent this condition of affairs" (quoted in Brecher 1972:85). Strength of "law," as Olney confided on another occasion, meant responding to the situation in Pullman with a "force which is overwhelming" (quoted in Wiebe 1967:92). Disregarding the penchant of late nineteenth-century presidents to stay on the sidelines of governmental operation (excepting exercise of their veto power), and over the objections of Governor John Altgeld of Illinois, Cleveland supported his attorney general by sending federal troops to help break the strike. Numerous other strikes drew a similar response. American society lowered itself to the use of brute power.[13]

Emerging in 1890, even as the nation whirled along the competitive route into violence, the Populist Party drew on its roots in the National Farmers' Alliance and Industrial Union. The Alliance attempted to radicalize cooperative buying and selling by giving them a *mass* foundation.[14] Initiated at the grass roots, the Alliance claimed by the late 1880s more than three thousand suballiances that reached into remote farming areas, particularly in Southern and Plains states.[15] Neither the Alliance nor its Populist offspring ever organized the majority of farming people. But other contemporary farmers' organizations attracted far fewer adherents (see Tontz 1964:145–150).

Late twentieth-century Americans, as Christopher Lasch has observed, can have a difficult time grasping the significance of nineteenth-century agrarian Populism because the latter-day citizens have seen the "populist" label get applied so indiscriminately to political figures along the whole gamut from Ronald Reagan to Jesse Jackson, that the term loses veracity in direct correlation with its increased volume in the Left-Right echo chamber. Historians themselves have prejudiced the perception of the agrarian campaign by frequently painting it as a reactionary, conservative force given to backward looking and nostalgic pining for an idyllic family farm that never existed. This prejudice could not be further from the truth. Agrarian Populism represented a realistic effort *both* to reach back into tradition for the moral criteria of reform *and* to aim forward with concrete proposals to reckon with the challenges of an industrial economy.[16]

First, Populist reformation consisted of attempts to uphold a public ethic grounded in widespread American "producer" morality. Producers were, in the popular imagination of Lincoln's producer republic, the worthy farmers, mechanics, and small entrepreneurs who contrasted with idle "speculators" and their kin among bankers, lawyers, and others who profited from the honest pursuits of the "producing classes."[17] Populists, then, looked to reappropriate for a new age the legacies of biblical and republican moralities. Thus their political activity in Kansas in 1890, for example, could be described as a "pentecost of politics," a "crusade," a "religious revival." And one of their renowned orators, James H. "Cyclone" Davis of Texas, could embrace that beacon of republican virtue, Thomas Jefferson, and declare in the name of the Virginian that business corporations flouted public accountability and subverted the good of the republic, exerting "influence... vast enough to shape the law of the government which created them."[18] Simultaneously, reflecting a tension that would later help to unravel the unity of the farmers' movement, Populism accepted liberal individualism and its Lockian limitations on any political action to control "private" enterprise. In the previous decade, the Supreme Court had determined—dubiously, to be sure—that corporations were "persons" entitled to due-process protection of privacy under the Fourteenth Amendment, thence setting the stage for Populists subsequently to founder on the dichotomy between the "rights" (interests) of private property and the public duty to restrain such claims.[19]

Second, marking the forward-looking approach of those concerned to face the challenges of industrialization, Populists promoted specific reforms aimed at securing social (moral) responsibility in the economy. Following the Populist national convention in St. Louis in 1892, a nominating convention that same year launched the Omaha Platform. Included in its comprehensive approach to the reform of American society were planks calling for government ownership of railroads, elimination of corporate land "speculation," and release from a financial system controlled by bankers.[20] The Platform intended to achieve an equitable distribution of resources in a "cooperative commonwealth."[21] This goal rested on the premise of "antimonopoly," the "principle," said Populist F. J. Ripley of Georgia, "that wealth belongs to him who creates it, rather than to those who by chicanery, legislation and fortuitous circumstances manage to get possession of it" (quoted in Palmer 1980:23). Such ideas soon found embodiment in the electoral successes of Populism, and the influence of the movement eventually stretched into forty-three states and territories (see Goodwyn 1976:chaps. 7, 11, pp. 323–343, 548, esp. 325–326).

As indicated above, Populists were torn between their own marketplace liberalism and the implications of reforms they advanced for meeting the problem of corporate power. On the one hand, in keeping with liberal regard for the autonomous freedom of private enterprise, a privacy now claimed by corporations as well, and for Lockian principles of limited government, many in the party feared the interventionism of the Omaha Platform and its overtones of socialism. On the other hand, collusive opposition from bankers and other businessmen had contributed to the failure of the "free" business ventures of Alliance cooperatives. Populists, therefore, frequently concluded that only the active government of the Platform could accomplish the initial aims of the Alliance. Ensuing division within the party undermined united action; by 1896 Populists were vulnerable to pressure to fuse with Democrats. But fusion eroded the comprehensive program of the Omaha Platform by directing Populist attention to the single issue of the free coinage of silver. The failure of that issue to catapult Democrats to victory in the presidential election of 1896 afforded a major reason for the subsequent decline of Populist fortunes.[22]

Regardless of disagreements among themselves, the agrarian reformers approached unanimity in understanding their movement to be a veritable last stand for a public morality in America that could span the chasm to the private realm, and therein construct reasonable constraints on the egoistic and chaotic pursuit of self-interest.[23] Already, in St. Louis in 1892, amid the period's accelerating national disintegration, the firebrand from Minnesota, Ignatius Donnelly, had rendered his picture of the disarray in his famous preamble to the Populist Platform: "We meet in the midst of a nation brought to the verge of moral, political, and material ruin. Corruption dominates the ballot box, the legislatures, the Congress, and touches even the ermine of the bench. The people are demoralized." To William Peffer of Kansas, corporations nurtured an ethos of acquisitiveness that translated into "a gigantic scheme of spoliation." In 1893 Georgia's Tom Watson pondered the corporation's assumption of "baronial right" to execute the arbitrary assertion of its power, and voiced his grief that "in all essential respects, the Republic of our fathers is dead. The remnants of its form, its outward semblance, may be left but its animating spirit is gone."[24]

After 1896 the republic remained dead. Marking Democratic capture and shrinkage of the Populist agenda to silver coinage, that date signified a watershed defeat of reformers' self-confidence, and the agrarian stride toward a public, American morality never recovered its former momentum.[25] In his classic study *The Decline of Agrarian*

Democracy, Grant McConnell observed that farmers' activism tended subsequently to avoid larger questions of public reconstruction and instead dwelled on issues of immediate concern, notably higher farm prices (see McConnell 1953:19, 39–43). Meanwhile, it became a commonplace for Americans to assume in succeeding years that "progressive" reform—consumer protection laws, financial innovations, electoral reforms—had set at rest the bad old days of Gilded-Age corruption and brutality masquerading as "law." But something more was afoot. Lawrence Goodwyn writes that after Populism the nation actually marched largely unimpeded in the direction of aggravating "the most difficult problem facing mankind: the centralization of power in highly technological societies."[26] Although "progressives" celebrated the achievement of the direct primary, the initiative, referendum, and other features of direct democracy, it was becoming ever more clear that effective power in the United States had scarcely anything to do with casting votes (cf. Goodwyn 1976:534–537).

Morality had failed in the political arena, and so it became important to get morality "out of politics." Of course, moral rhetoric, and in particular the muckraking attacks on corporations, continued to arouse civic indignation. The corporation, after all, was a greater influence than ever before. Corporate consolidation rushed ahead, and a billow of mergers from 1897 to 1903 produced forty industrial companies possessing more than $50 million in capital. At the earlier date there had been merely eight. Each year between 1895 and 1905, larger entities swallowed some three hundred independent enterprises. By 1919 concerns with over $1 million of annual output constituted just 3.6 percent of all firms, but they employed 56.9 percent of the nation's workers and generated 67.8 percent of American manufacturing production. But remedies for the moral problem of disproportionate corporate

power seemed invariably to involve establishment of centralized bureaucracies—exemplified especially by the
Federal Reserve System initiated in 1913 and by the
Federal Trade Commission of 1914—whose legitimacy was
anchored in the authority of the appointed expert who
would be impartial and aloof from the unresolved tangles of
morality while regulating affairs in the name of efficient
management. If the notion of *interest* had proved to be hos-
tile to morality, that of *efficiency* would prove to be indifferent to it.[27]

The word *efficiency* was central to understanding why
the republic was dead and hence why public morality had
vanished. In his examination of developments around the
turn of the twentieth century, Samuel Haber noted that
homage to efficient practice reached such magnitude in the
United States as to constitute "a secular Great Awakening"
(Haber 1964:ix–x). It was expected that a normal citizen
would extol the business or commercial efficiency of a
favorable balance sheet, the mechanical and technical
efficiency of a properly managed individual plant, the
economic efficiency of a productive order, and the social
efficiency of harmonious relations that competent
experts generated through sophisticated technique. In a
word, the nation more and more incarnated a Newtonian
conception of the world and cosmos as functionally sub-
divided, harmoniously interconnected, and delightedly
open to exact measurement, prediction, and control. In
this world, morality (with its concomitant teleological
implications) was irrelevant. What mattered was that
Enlightenment science grasped the cause-and-effect relations of natural laws; that is, that scientists learned to
manipulate the domain of facts. It mattered also that society could be viewed as a feature of nature, as a real object
of measurement in factual terms, and hence as a location
for the extension of scientific manipulation. Competent
manipulators, moreover, did not arrive at their competence

by demonstrating their worth in republican elections. This demonstration, instead, increasingly entailed getting a Ph.D. degree in a technical discipline hosted by a meritorious university.[28]

So, for example, in this culture of expertise the conservation movement offered to regulate the public domain by centralizing control of natural-resource technology and by having government approximate an Olympian supervision over the various users of nature's bounty. To W. J. McGee, geologist and chief conservation theorist, this supervisory role meant overcoming the chaotic consequences of reliance on laissez-faire practices and instituting multiple-purpose resource management. Such administration involved, in particular, a conception of rivers not only as a vehicle of transportation but as a means for irrigation and production of hydroelectric power as well. Waterways became "an interrelated system" whose "several parts" formed a totality under the mastery of the technologist. "It is in this concept of the river as a power to be controlled by engineering projects" that McGee again and again found a basis for arguing the importance of "entering into control over nature... for the direct benefit of mankind." This centralized technical management, he concluded, meant that "the perfect machine... is the fruit of the ages."[29] McGee's thinking reflected a mainstream fixation on technological command that infused one reform effort after another, including everything from the reclamation projects out of the national Department of the Interior, to the initial efforts to establish city commission and manager forms of government (see Pisani 1983:53–58; and Wiebe 1967:170).

Re-formation at the behest of bureaucratic organization, then, drew its legitimacy from the scientific capacity to harness the technology that promised, on the one hand, to restore order—that is, control—to a fractured nation. With this prospect in mind, Arthur Hadley, economist and later the president of Yale, noted that social science showed to administrators "how the largely independent action of the parts may be made to conduce to the collective good of the whole." Whereas, because "the practical workings of representative government" served diverse local districts and party interests, it resulted "that the collective action of the whole is made to fulfill the separate wants of the parts" (quoted in Skowronek 1982:160–161; see also Wiebe 1967:152, 160–163). Here by implication the expert's justification resided both in mastering the techniques that would produce efficient sociality and in disengaging from messy fights over particularist "values."

On the other hand, while bureaucracy fed on collective disorder by contending that it could secure needed integration, fledgling technocracy also trumpeted rhetoric about efficiency in order to declare that technocrats staffed the agencies of progress and thus possessed the effective means of material abundance. Echoing McGee, Simon Patten, whose thinking in *The New Basis of Civilization* would later influence the New Deal, announced that human "dominion over nature" would stop the "reign of want." Undoubtedly, "The social surplus is the superlative machine brought forth in the machine age for the quickening of progress" (quoted in Lasch 1991:69). Intellectual optimism such as this fortified bureaucracy to proclaim that under its aegis the future would consist of endless—not to be confused with purposeful—improvement. Posterity would simply have the power to acquire more.[30]

Francis Bacon had realized that "knowledge is power," that scientific induction generated the capability to control and manipulate. In twentieth-century America, technical application of Baconian method legitimized the centralized power of those who motioned to effect order where there had been none, and who justified bureaucratic centralization by arguing that it would empower everyone else to partake of "the good life" of material plenty. But aimless acquisition suggested the vacuity at the heart of American culture. Where was "more" going? Answering this question required moral resolution that could no longer be achieved in public life.

In sum, the pursuit of individual freedom did not finish where antebellum proponents of commercial independence had hoped it would. Instead of securing proprietary self-sufficiency, the unfettered marketplace charted a trajectory through fierce competition, corporate consolidation, depression, and chaos, until, finally, regulatory bureaucracy traded the promise of material abundance for power to constrain freedom in the name of necessary order. Along the way biblical and republican ideas of the collective good did not survive as forces able to determine the shape of public affairs. Constituting the last movement in American history with a realistic chance to re-form the social totality—especially the economy—to cohere with those traditional ideas,[31] agrarian Populism foundered on internal contradictions and on pressures in 1896 to fuse with Democrats. Thereafter the foundation was laid in government policy for technical experts to pose (their!) bureaucratic organization as the only power able to restrain laissez-faire devolution into brutishness. The public became the realm of objective "facts" where only specialized expertise could govern; the private domain became the repository of "values" that people could choose to embrace provided no one seriously thought that subjective beliefs might actually structure the administration of power. Hence the ruling order in America came to terms with morality by partitioning it off from the process of rule.

None of this is to say, of course, that there cannot be renewed efforts to establish some kind of biblical or republican hegemony. (There has, for example, been much concern expressed over the decay of the American polity, and thus considerable attention given to revitalizing a "civic humanism" able to stress communal "citizenship" [see

Lasch 1991:170–172].) Rather, the point is that by the early decades of the twentieth century the former traditions retained nothing approaching a commanding position. The forms and rituals of religious and republican activity could remain in motion, but, as Tom Watson had understood, that did not mean they were alive. As an index of this death, later in the century intellectuals could re-view Populism as a fantastic, preposterous effort at "imposing moral order on the market economy" (David Montgomery quoted in Lasch 1991:222). Such morality had become unthinkable. Not surprisingly, then, a glance in the direction of the historical typology of David Riesman and his co-authors could disclose yet another evacuation of moral sense. That is, one could read Riesman and company and surmise that the "inner-directed," guilt-ridden individualist of the nineteenth century had become in the twentieth the "other-directed" chameleon who confused morality with winning peer-group approval, who labored to build a résumé rather than a character, and who gravitated to bureaucratic mass media for direction that could no longer be found in a moral center (see Riesman, Glazer, and Denney 1953:esp. pt. 1).

Alasdair MacIntyre's concept of "bureaucratic individualism" captures and summarizes the heart of the foregoing history. He detects that individual freedom quarrels with bureaucracy over what will have sovereignty: "free and arbitrary choices" or "collectivist control." The fight between them is intense, but underneath the conflict is a "deep cultural agreement," a symbiotic dependence on each other based on a shared *raison d'être.*

Individualism finds its reason for being in the proclamation of liberty from bureaucratic regimentation. Collectivism locates its reason for being in the need to limit the chaos that would result if the cacophony of self-interest operated without constraint. But each grounds itself in nothing other than the will to dominate, to empower.

Individualism wants to be autonomous and free from manipulation, but in order to realize what it wants it must seek to get what it refuses to let anything else have—control. It goes to war. Collectivism boldly declares that it will stop the war, cohere the order, and deliver the goods; but otherwise it functions without purpose because it splits morality from the supposed objectivity that executes the multiyear plan. It throws its regulatory weight around. One contemplates this liberty-restriction symbiosis and wonders if perpetual recourse to the police is sufficient in the end for the task of founding a civilization.[32]

After the Second World War: Cultural Disintegration and Final Reliance on Bureaucratic Technique

Regardless of the extent of Christian influence on the formation of American identity (through, say, Great Awakening revivalism), it is doubtful whether Americans ever possessed a consistent "civil religion." They never accepted Christianity as a state religion. Nor did they ever make citizenship contingent upon compliance with a collection of religious beliefs.[33] But in the ideation and social practice of post–World War II American culture, it appeared for an ephemeral moment as if there might actually be a resurrection of a somewhat Christian public morality.

This moralism represented, more broadly, an amorphous Judeo-Christian belief in the godly mission of the United States to be a bastion of righteousness and democracy in a world menaced, among other things, by the totalitarian specter of communism. During the years around 1950, Americans hailed the arrival of their nation as the world's most powerful instrument of divine will. President Harry Truman declared that American citizens "shall not relent in our effort to bring the Golden Rule into the international affairs of the world." Not only this self-congratulatory confidence but an intense fear drove Americans to people the religious bulwarks lest democratic sanctity be overrun by godless communists (with Senator Joseph McCarthy eventually proving to be exceptionally sensitive to this spread), by return of the economic woes of the Great Depression, by the nightmare recurrence of war, and by moral decadence in the wake of resurgent consumer materialism. One mother wrote in *Bible Magazine* of her anxiety that children might inherit a future where they are "driven through the streets to an unknown but horrible fate." Alas, she concluded, "We desire for our children a normal life." A Jewish anecdote told of the telegram received from a friend: "Start worrying. Letter follows." Religious observance became essential to the establishment of a sense of normalcy.[34]

The institutions of organized religion benefited from the Americanism that presumed God to be at once the source of national power and the security against global calamity. Budgets, building programs, and membership rolls expanded rapidly. The Disciples of Christ, for example, pointed to their biggest yearly member advances in more than thirty years. During immediate postwar years, Catholics annually celebrated a million infant baptisms. From 1946 to 1949, the Southern Baptist Convention listed five hundred church starts, costing $97 million. And on it went; one organization after another bulged the latest numerical increase. Franklin Fry of the United Lutheran Church gave voice to the heady experience when he said, "We have risen into the atmosphere at last. It has been a tingling revelation of hidden power." Other religious leaders clasped the historical moment of confidence and anxiety and saw religion once more as a significant influence on public life. Echoing a chorus of similar views, Harry Emerson Fosdick believed God was summoning everyone to the difficult task of "getting something done on earth to redeem our race from its sin and misery." It was time for synagogues and churches to lend a hand in saving the world.[35]

Representatives of these organizations considered, however, that in America their suasion rested on the widely shared assumption that culture constituted the "values" that shaped conduct, and in turn religion formed the best way to assure proper valuation. Hence, as Robert Wuthnow observes, many in the late 1940s and early 1950s argued that "religion's impact on cultural values was the mainstay of good morals, democracy, and social order" (Wuthnow 1988:59; see also 63). In 1946 Senator Wayne Morse was not alone in the kind of reasoning that led him in particular to propose that the truths of the Lord's Prayer should form a personal code guiding each member of Congress regarding action pertaining to labor legislation. The postwar years resounded, in other words, with the idea that a religious institution comprised a "fellowship" based on the pious devotion of individuals. The fellowship's purpose was to nurture the values that individuals (*as* individuals) could impress upon civic life. "The great thing Jesus did for us," the prominent Baptist W. A. Criswell of Texas maintained, "was to set forth the worth of the individual" and to work "upon the principle that society derives its life from the individuals who compose it."[36] So long as there remained some measure of agreement respecting the constitution of "good morals," this privatization of religious judgment could claim to translate indirectly into responsible public action (see Wuthnow 1988:65–67).

Social commentators of the period made much of American consensus (see, e.g., Hartz 1955); yet it was precisely moral agreement that proved to be ephemeral. If one followed Martin E. Marty's reasoning, this ephemerality probably stemmed from the shallowness of the contemporary revivalism. People did not engage in renewal from the wellsprings of their faith traditions. Instead, as Marty contended, there was merely a "revival of *interest* in religion" (Marty 1958 59:10). By the 1960s it became clear that a public—that is, a shared American, a governing—morality had resurrected only in appearance. Divisions erupted over the Vietnam War and the ongoing civil rights movement. (Did moral conduct still signify the indirect influence exerted on government by an individual's personal code? Or did it entail a direct action campaign for social justice?) The 1960s marked, moreover, something of a mushroom takeoff for a welter of exotic religious persuasions that had been gradually developing on American soil—Muslim, Hindu, Buddhist, and sundry sectarian attachments. (If, in such a "pluralist" environment, the nation was to have a public morality, whose name would underwrite the moral norm?) Indeed, the proliferation of "new" faith perspectives compounded with geographic and socioeconomic mobility to loosen older denominational ties. Contemporaries witnessed the increasing emergence of a preferential world where one might either opt to be a secularist without definite religious orientation, or prefer to be affiliated with "special agenda organizations" whose interests ranged across a gamut of politico-religious concerns. Whatever developments in morality lay ahead, they would transpire without the denominational anchorage of the 1950s.[37]

There unfolded in ensuing years, in struggles over abortion, gay rights, and the like, what James Davison Hunter helpfully described as "culture wars." As tempting as it was, however, to view these as battles between Left and Right, modern and antimodern, liberal and conservative, or (in Hunter's nomenclature) progressive and orthodox forces, it did not appear to be helpful to rely on the explanatory power of these categories. There were "wars" all right, but not between two polar camps. Amid the miasma created by such categorization, it became more difficult to see clearly that neither side of the supposed polarity constituted enough internal coherence to represent a consistent adversary. On the Right, for example, paralleling the fractious inconsistency of nineteenth-century agrarian Populism, there was the incompatible marriage of a biblical communalism with a liberal marketplace individualism. On the Left, meanwhile, there were marriages of convenience combining social democratic collectivism ("justice") and civil libertarian individuality. (One might imagine Marx and Engels gasping at the naiveté of the latter union!) Although one could, following Hunter, discern broad "*impulses* or *tendencies*" toward polarization between traditional verity versus relativist fluidity, in reality, as Alasdair MacIntyre suggested, groups of people, at once in need of rhetorical legitimacy and unconscious of their moral predicament, were grabbing fragments of this or that valuational heritage, thence fighting less to advance unitary liberal or conservative platforms and more just to satisfy their particular agendas.[38]

Whatever else was said about cultural warfare, one thing was incontestable: Different sides based respective actions on incompatible foundations of moral authority. Protestant, Catholic, Mormon, and other groups invoked the revealed authority of various Scriptures. Others, given to a kind of transcendent orientation but indisposed to believe in the diverse deities, slugged it out on behalf of a perception of social order as grounded in the natural rationality or natural law derived from a classical humanism. Still others would dismiss transcendence and follow the autonomous rationality rooted in "Enlightenment naturalism" exemplified by Thomas Hobbes and expressed through empirical method. And yet untold others, perhaps wearied by the incessant, confusing, and mounting discord, took refuge in the inner sanctum of authoritative subjectivity and therein relied on their own personal experience. Although he tried to translate this multisided battle as a two-pronged affair, Hunter nonetheless accurately surveyed the divisions, borrowed Emile Durkheim's classification of the sacred as anything humans exalt, and arrested attention with the observation: "Not only does each side of the cultural divide operate with a different conception of the sacred, but the mere existence of the one represents a certain desecration of the other."[39] It could have been added that such "desecration" had always and typically accompanied processes of cultural disintegration. In a word, the nation unfolded a later stage of a long development that W. B. Yeats had already stamped with the often quoted lines: "Things fall apart; the centre cannot hold; / Mere anarchy is loosed upon the world" (quoted in Ellmann 1948:233).

By the late 1980s the reality of American disintegration could be seen on many fronts. Whose right would determine whether the unborn child should remain so? whether homosexuality contradicted natural order? whether public schooling ought to acknowledge revealed truth? Disintegration, the inability to be together, was shown in the lack of collectively accepted answers to questions such as these. Although representing an arena of no greater importance than many others, and though often generating hyperbole disproportional to actual influence on national events, the arts and entertainment industry effectively allegorized the nation's condition.[40] When, for example, Andres Serrano used the modest and indirect support of the National Endowment for the Arts to tender *Piss Christ*, his photographic exhibit of a cross in a container of his own urine, the opportunity for hyperbolical reaction did not go unexploited. Critics transformed minimal subsidy into, "Is this how you want your tax dollars spent?"[41] In 1989 the rap group 2 Live Crew found over two hundred occasions on a single album to say the word *fuck*, and entered a region of controversy familiar to Serrano. Defenders of these artists relied on the right to individual expression of the individual quest to understand individual experience. If one wondered why this "right" should be honored, it might be rebutted that there was a natural, obvious, self-evident reason for 2 Live Crew to be *As Nasty As They Wanna Be*. Obvious to whom? Self-evident on the basis of what authority? Individual egos varied considerably and, depending on the slant of the one or the other, there were no rational grounds for expressiveness to stop short of "Piss Buddha," or "Piss Gandhi," or "Piss It All." Extreme art, then, symbolized the turn toward a nation that demanded tolerance of everything and hence imposed nihilism on everyone. Defenders of "community standards" ironically accelerated the whirl of disintegration by posing authoritarian censorship—exemplified by occasional instances of police and other harassment of performers and by closure of arts facilities, thence portending to root "order" in the kind of regime that produces rebellious chaos in the form of expressive "pissing." On all sides of American cultural division people increasingly divorced will from reason and pursued the imposition of respective righteousness. Here was a twist on Friedrich Nietzsche: He had hoped the will to power would be the principle of creative self-realization that would redeem Western history from descent into nothingness. Americans, however, confirmed that such willfulness established right through one or another variety of destructive force.[42] By 1991 Christopher Lasch announced that contending factions had "exhausted" their moral capital (Lasch 1991:21). There was no public morality in America. But Tom Watson had realized this in 1893.

American government had already tried for many years to manage cultural disintegration by erecting a wall between neutral governance and unresolvable partisan bickering. The official separation of public from private afforded an exact parallel to René Descartes' philosophical project that eventuated in separating objective and subjective ways of grasping the world, the former being the region of unarguable "facts" and the latter constituting the domain of disputable "beliefs" (see Descartes 1951). Americans demonstrated this division when they sought to separate state from church. The demonstration reached a high watermark in 1971 when the Supreme Court considered, in *Lemon v. Kurtzman*, whether a state program could help finance the cost of materials and salaries in private and religious schools. The Court decided that such help was unconstitutional, issuing the "Lemon test" for determining whether statutes concurred with the Establishment Clause of the Constitution: "First, the statute must have a secular legislative purpose; second, its principal or primary effect must be one that neither advances nor inhibits religion...; finally, the statute must not foster 'an excessive government entanglement with religion'" (quoted in Carter 1993:110). The Court mandated "a secular legislative purpose" that aimed to compartmentalize religion from public life. Any judicial failure to observe this "secular" line risked exploding the fragile foundation of American order that, on the subjective side, resided in allowing the privatized exploration of what Stephen L. Carter called "God as a hobby," while, on the objective side, inhered in permitting bureaucratic organization to perform without the handicap of needing to know whether God sanctioned the policy.[43] Fortunately, the ambiguous nature of "excessive government entanglement" opened legal room to maneuver for the drawing and redrawing of a line that remained tenuous because it encoded the fracture of the body politic.

In lieu of agreement in the supposed inward moral sphere, after the Second World War Americans—hardly prevented by the ephemeral moralism of the late 1940s and 1950s—fixated on outward indicators of "real" success like being "number one" in the won-loss columns, having more consumer products to choose from, and achieving all the bigger and better results of an effective technological society whose abundance served usually to quell fears that quantitative measurement by itself was pointless (cf. Wuthnow 1988:261, 268, 276–277; see also n. 33 above). The apprehensions were significant for the fixation culminated in apparent indifference to the worth of life itself. During the Vietnam War, for example, the Defense

Department sought to conduct the conflict through the instruments of systems analysis and statistical management. These required calculation according to ratio of cost to benefit. The Department thus issued instruction cards to soldiers for the purpose of establishing precise rules for engaging enemy and civilian populations. The Enemy in Your Hands card, for instance, specified five rules, ranging from truism ("Take the captive quickly to security.") to delusional loss of contact with the soldier's reality ("All persons in your hands, whether suspects, civilians, or combat captives must be protected against violence, insults, curiosity, and reprisals of any kind" [quoted in Stivers 1994:78].). However absurd, the cards reflected the Department's effort to operationalize and to make measurable its emphasis on productivity. War-managers aimed for similar measurability through focus on "body count" (the ratio of American and allied Vietnamese dead to enemy Vietnamese or Viet Cong dead). Promotions came to hinge on body-count production, and pressure mounted for higher and higher counts, until soldiers reduced theorized rules of enemy-civilian engagement to one actual rule, the "'Mere Gook Rule': 'If it's dead and it's Vietnamese, it's VC'" (quoted in Stivers 1994:78).

Here was a bureaucratic course of action that offered to assert technical control and quantitative success as the only things to value in the end. Power, the requisite for succeeding, got absolutized, and the depth of American rule rose to the surface to shatter especially the faith of many Vietnam veterans who once trusted the nation.[44] Writing of the type of rationality characteristic of this historical process of absolutization of power, Max Weber had fixed on the age-old bureaucratic rationalization that was intensified by the large-scale administration of modern capitalism and wedded to efficient *means* for the manipulation of natural and human material. Weber observed that management organized to administer the centrally directed hierarchy of functionally specialized and rationally coordinated personnel, who operated according to precise and impersonal rules while advancing "careers" on the basis of formal qualifications. Amid this intensification of administered organization, moral *ends* became irrelevant to the bureaucratized consciousness preoccupied with authority resident solely in effectiveness derived from manipulative techniques for the mastery of others.[45]

Scholars have made an industry of referring to empirical inaccuracies in Weber's analysis of bureaucracy, but historical development corroborated Weberian observations regarding the tendency of the West to unfold in an "iron cage" of bureaucratic structures whose only authoritative rationale was amoral effectiveness (see MacIntyre 1984:26, 86, 109, 114). In America one sensed the weight of bureaucracy merely by noting that in 1980 agencies of federal administration generated approximately 100,000 pages of rules. Had it factored in the regulations produced, say, by bureaucratized business corporations, the number would have mounted still higher (see Stivers 1994:75). William G. Scott and David K. Hart saw in such proliferation the signs of an "organizational imperative" that subsumed the individual's aspirations under a drive for the maintenance, growth, and general health of organizations, and that veered in the "totalitarian" direction of acquiring sufficient means of control to ensure total conformity with large-scale objectives (see Scott and Hart 1979:43–48, 207–214). Notwithstanding the bureaucratic concern to establish rules that sounded vaguely moral, these, as Jacques Ellul persistently reminded, embodied the fact that Western societies increasingly structured themselves as a totality or environment of instrumental techniques focused (in all operational fields) on the requisition of efficiency, and bureaucratic regulations were simply a prime manifestation of this technicism. *Rules* spread as a *means* to be efficient while taking moral *ends* as pre-set generalities outside the purview of the agency's technicist rationality.[46] Weber himself had thought of just one way to avoid the sealed enclosure of the amoral system: "Only by reversion in every field-political, religious, economic, etc.—to small-scale organization would it be possible to any considerable extent to escape its [bureaucracy's] influence" (Weber 1947:338).

In the midst of the bureaucratization, Americans developed individualist strategies that tried to carve out private space for self-expression. After the rugged competition-*cum*-nervous exhaustion of nineteenth-century market-place competitiveness, individualism instanced mutations not only into the counsel of Norman Vincent Peale and others to heal and renew through the positive thinking that internalized manipulative technique as self-mastery, but also into ever more exaggerated varieties of solipsism that knew only an interior source of truth in the self.[47] For example, regarding the last-mentioned, in their remarkable encounter in the 1980s with a nurse, Sheila Larson, Robert N. Bellah and his colleagues, in *Habits of the Heart*, found that this woman believed in "Sheilaism," in her "own little voice" that said to her, "Just try to love yourself and be gentle with yourself" (quoted in Bellah 1985:221; see also 235). In tandem with developing a private set of beliefs, one could seek meaning through consumption of a "lifestyle," through the vicarious drama of film and television, or through the psychotherapy that seemed to find its *raison d'être* in compensating for bureaucracy's impersonality. But none of these individual strategies challenged the presuppositions of social organization based on bureaucratic technique; Americans now relied on the latter to keep the nation functioning.[48]

In sum, after the Second World War the religious-moral revival that followed World War II in the 1940s and 1950s proved to be superficial enough to fracture at the first significant experiences of social division in the 1960s.

Cultural disintegration ensued as Americans whirled into multiple belief perspectives that offered incompatible answers to the chief questions of the day. Public morality failed, and government redoubled the effort to draw a secular line between private (religious) and public (state) spheres, a line itself signifying a deeply divided nation. The national order relied finally on bureaucratic technique that pursued efficiency while remaining indifferent to moral ends.

Robert Wuthnow observed that its mire in conflict yielded American religion's increasing inability to provide "the broad, consensual underpinnings of societal legitimation." This deficiency led in turn to a growing reliance on technology as "a vast institution" or "basic feature of modern life" whose tangible impact on society was "more objective than God" (Wuthnow 1988:226, 282, 286). It could have been added that dependence on technique amounted both to the efficient pursuit of success as an end in itself, and hence to the exaltation of the power to succeed. (Americans might have recalled William James's reflection on their worship of the bitch-goddess SUCCESS.) Not surprisingly, as Richard Stivers suggested, people became more and more cynical as they sensed behind every idealistic proclamation a clever exercise of someone's will-to-manipulate-for-advantage.[49]

Unless some way could be found to recover humanity from the inhumanity of an amoral culture,[50] the future took on the cast to which MacIntyre alluded: "Pessimism too will turn out to be one more cultural luxury that we shall have to dispense with in order to survive in these hard times" (MacIntyre 1984:5). The Enlightenment's autonomous technical reason, stripped of moral teleology and divorced from the holy, had led the nation into spiritual emptiness. The widely versed Christian missionary, Lesslie Newbigin, pointed to the meaninglessness induced by the West's anomic separation of morality from the public sphere. This tear caused the collapse of a shared sense of the *good* and prompted Newbigin to assert that "Jürgen Moltmann is surely right when he says that over the developed and afflu-ent Western societies there seems to hang the banner: 'No Future'" (Newbigin 1989:111–112, see also 90–91, 218, 101, 223). Now matters were clear; American culture too had no hope.

Wisdom for Post-Enlightenment Culture: Ecclesiastes

Writing under the enigmatic Hebrew designation as "Qoheleth" (which possibly meant a personal name, a nickname, an acronym, or an official instructional activi-ty), the author of Ecclesiastes summoned attention to the experience of life as meaningless futility: "Vanity of vani-ties, says the Teacher, vanity of vanities! All is vanity" (1:2).[51] Qoheleth applied all his powers of observation "to seek and to search out by wisdom all that is done under heaven; it is an unhappy business that God has given to human beings to be busy with" (1:13). God's inscrutable will rendered human effort pointless; attainment of great wisdom (contra-Proverbs) went unrewarded; pursuit of pleasure proved vacuous; both the wise and fools came to death and to the portion of being forgotten—all leading Qoheleth to the conclusion that "I hated life, because what is done under the sun was grievous to me; for all is vanity and a chasing after wind" (2:17; see also 1:14–2:16, 18–26; 9:16).

Ecclesiastes took on the appearance of unremitting unhappiness over everything in the created order. The famous poem in the third chapter stated that all things have their moment, but Qoheleth seemed to add the point that people were too blind to see what occasion God was now offering them (3:1–8, 11). Injustice triumphed over justice, and humans met the same fate as animals (3:16–19; 8:14). Wealth was difficult to secure and in the end could not satisfy (5:10–20). A lot of things were better than other things—exemplified by the obvious superiority of patience over pride—but God's unchangeable will was that the better could not eradicate the worse, and hence it was better to mourn than to be festive (7:1–14). Random chance governed and so destroyed the possibility of any certain reward for virtue (9:11–12). Regardless of the respective merits of groups or individuals, death represented an evil reduction of them all to a kind of unjust sameness (9:1–3, 10). In the end, as in the beginning, "Vanity of vanities, says the Teacher; all is vanity" (12:8).

Qoheleth, in other words, wanted to convey to the listener the full impact of what it was like to live in a self-centered, one-dimensional world sealed off from the possibility of God's gracious transformation. Thus, in his observations early in Ecclesiastes, the Teacher established the echo of the self-absorbed refrain: "I saw… I have acquired… I applied… I perceived… I searched… I made… I bought… I got…" (1:14 2:8ff.). By the time of the fourth chapter the Teacher considered that companionship surpassed loneliness because the companion enhanced *Qoheleth's* consolation (4:9 12). In the self-centered world there was no doubt that *I* was even more bereft if I lacked kinship with others, such that "I saw vanity under the sun: the case of solitary individuals, without sons or brothers" (4:7–8a).

Hence, through ironic posturing as a self-enclosed ego, Qoheleth has moved us to see the consequence of basing life on the autonomous "I": The outcome was meaninglessness. Note again his meditation: "So I turned to consider wisdom and madness and folly" (2:12a). This search, he found, led the I straight to the reality of its status as creature, unable to comprehend the mystery of God's action. Yet, given to an overweening sense of self-importance, the I persisted in believing that it was a creator, but discovered that its actions changed nothing. Alas, "That which is, already has been; that which is to be, already is" (3:15). As long as the I insisted that it knew how to exploit the power to remake the order of things, its activity would eventuate exclusively in meaninglessness.[52]

In the aftermath of the failure of the American project to build a civilization on the foundation of the Enlightenment's autonomous (I) rationality, we see about us the descent of decadent modernity into "postmodern" criticism that pushes Cartesian doubt (the principle that nothing is exempted from skeptical query) to its logical finale: self-consumption, implosion into an emptiness unable to affirm any truth at all. This critical I still clings to autonomy; only now in aggregation with others, it has become, in keeping with suggestions like Michel Foucault's true-through-imposition "regimes of truth," a cacophonous "we" of plural viewpoints whose signal common characteristic is inability to be together. Americans are lonely. The loneliness has metastasized into contest for power, a disintegration that Nietzsche recognized in the West and Newbigin translated thus: "Violence is the fundamental element of human life and history."[53] Qoheleth had already seen that claims to human creativity-cum-self-sufficiency led to nothing but vanity, to the void. But he retained hope that if the true Creator de-centered human autonomy, in the full stride of what youth people had, they might yet discover much that God wanted them to do (cf. 11:9; 12:1). We now turn to examples of ecclesial practice that have perhaps excelled at what God did not want them to do.

3

Into the Vacuum:
Disestablishment and "Mainline" Protestant Failure

Establishment, Disestablishment, and "Decline"

It might be taken as axiomatic that identifying—to the point of fusion—with an American culture in dissolution would bring trouble to churches who pursue this identification. "Mainline" Protestant bodies (Episcopalians, Presbyterians, Methodists, and the like), who merit their "mainstream" classification not because they exert a main effect on the current normative structures of society but because of their historic ties either to the nation's revolutionary beginnings or to its frontier development, have demonstrated the plausibility of this axiom. Denominational trouble evidences to those who are aware that membership in these denominations has been declining more or less steadily for over twenty-five years. One can, of course, get distracted from recognizing the implications of this deterioration by sinking instead into the mire of defensive huffing, puffing, and arguing over the nature of the "decline"—contending that the decrease stems from retaliation for expressions of "prophetic" courage in the mainline churches, or that it involves an organic and necessary process of death and rebirth, or even that it really is not happening because membership data read unevenly across denominations while religious involvement in America remains relatively high and potentially available for Protestant replenishment.[1] Here, however, we will explore the course set by our axiom.

There is no doubt that mainstream Protestants blended thoroughly with prevailing tendencies in the surrounding culture. In American church history, for example, especially after the Civil War the formation of denominational bureaucracies accelerated. Before the War extralocal Christian activity divided between denominations concerned, on the one hand, to discipline membership in the requirements of the faith, and voluntary associations (the American Bible Society founded in 1816, the American Sunday-School Union in 1824, etc.) who aimed, on the other hand, to administer affairs by raising funds, investing endowments, preparing educational curricula, publishing hymnbooks, and so on. After the War denominations gradually absorbed and transformed the independent societies into denominational departments or divisions. (A Sunday School association, say, became a denomination's bureau of religious education.) As the ecclesiastical hierarchies expanded in the direction of bureaucratic administration, they relaxed older concerns for member discipline and instead devoted themselves to efficient management of resources.[2] Presbyterians, affording a crystal instance of the trend, watched as their concern for organizational records waxed while their practice of extended worship services waned (see Weeks 1991:112). Conrad Wright insists: "For an understanding of what was going on, Max Weber is a more helpful guide than the Apostle Paul" (Wright 1984:185). Indeed, in their desire to incorporate the functions of the voluntary associations, the denominations emulated the way business corporations gobbled independent entrepreneurs. Protestants might continue over time to indulge the egalitarian rhetoric of the "priesthood of all believers," but ecclesiastical power looked very centralized and inegalitarian in practice. One could apply the typology of H. Richard Niebuhr and see in this bureaucratization the development of a "Christ of culture" in bureaucratic form.[3]

It made sense for mainline Protestants to organize themselves to blend with the predominant organizational pattern of the wider culture. Although Americans never accepted Christianity as a state religion, nor as a part of a state-imposed code of religious beliefs that hinged citizenship on compliance with fixed tenets, still, as Douglas John Hall has emphasized, mainstream Protestantism played an important role in forming a de facto "cultural establishment" based on the like-minded church-nation self-understanding exemplified in respect both for worship attendance as integral to, though not formally required for, being a citizen, and for Christianity as a historic bulwark of advancing Western civilization.[4] Loren B. Mead, in *The Once and Future Church*, speaks similarly of "Christendom" as a "paradigm" for showing the assumptions undergirding the quasi-Christian nation—that is, for manifesting, among other things, why Christian mission has been constructed as a far-off adjunct to the spread of American "democracy," why clergy donned roles as "chaplains" who conceived of congregations as territorial parishes, and why pastors fulfilled the chaplaincy by consenting to "do" baptisms and weddings regardless of the religious preparation of the *citizens* seeking these tokens of Christian "service" (see Mead 1991:14–18, 20–25, 33, 84). As implied in Chapter 1, Christendom supplied the organist (whose name was *legion!*) with the taken-for-granted assumption that songs appropriate to Memorial Day patriotism overrode the selection of hymns suited to Pentecost Sunday—a presupposition equivalent to saying that the church *believed what the civic community believed.* So, again, as influential partners in this culturally established order of things, Protestants acted as if by second nature when they assumed the bureaucratic shape of the nation that provided them with a favorable habitat.

By the end of the twentieth century in North America, however, denominational achievements of bureaucracy proceeded to disintegrate under the impact of a seismic and ongoing shift in church history. The change might be termed the "deconstantinianization" of Christianity (that is, the end of the habit of equating the ruling regime with the foremost embodiment of God's historical activity), the "disestablishment" of Christendom, or, in Albert van den Heuvel's striking nomenclature, "the humiliation of the church" (quoted in Hall 1989:24). However worded, the signal fact remained that quasi-Christian nationalism increasingly evaporated amidst the multiplication of competing faith perspectives and the downscaling of Christianity to be but one voice among many on a social landscape characterized by privatization of belief, and by what Hall called "the rapid growth of an almost complete religionlessness on the part of many" (Hall n.d.:9–10; see also Hall 1989:50–59). Once a guarantor of public morality, mainline Protestantism now met a culture lacking shared moral sense, a supermarket-like environment in which common loyalty found itself defeated by the plural "choices" of a get-what-you-want individualistic freedom (see Roof and McKinney 1987:40–52).

Having tied church growth to large-scale and efficient accumulation of wealth, property, members, and social influence, mainstream Protestants presently encountered a stunning reversal of fortune as denominations experienced substantial losses in all these respects. Since the 1960s, for example, the unfolding trend was membership drops for every denomination, including some denominational bodies who exited each decade with at least 10 percent fewer members than they had coming in.[5] By one early 1980s estimate, "White Westerners cease to be practicing Christians at a rate of 7,600 per day" (Barrett quoted in

Hall n.d.:9). Another account summarized the situation by noting that "the current malaise" in the mainline traditions warranted approaching the matter of decline "as a study in pathology" (Coalter, Mulder, and Weeks 1992:25). The very array of the denominations—as the plural "brands" of Christian religion—enabled them willy-nilly to mirror the privatized cultural supermarket, to feed into the privatization that destroyed public morality while consequently toppling these same Protestant bodies who used to help secure that moralism (see Newbigin 1994:64). Notwithstanding the theocratic efforts of certain ecclesiastical elements to restore Christendom, the age of disestablishment, the final unraveling of the Constantinian-Theodosian Establishment is well under way, and our axiom remains plausible: It might be taken as self-evident that identifying, to the point of fusion, with an American culture in dissolution would bring trouble to churches who pursue this identification.[6]

A Pastor's Urgent Bulletin from the Vacuum: Dying of Boredom

In my pastoral experience there was more involved in decline than broad historical tendencies. As important as these were as a shaping context for what I experienced with my congregations, and though history often determined our behavior in ways escaping our consciousness, there still remained an irreducible sense in which we were responsible for our decisions. I learned from my experience that church deterioration originates not only from the pressure of external historical forces but also from internal actions related to the integrity of mainline Protestants themselves. I found myself unable to avoid, though I desired very much to do so, the conclusions reached in a range of contemporary ecclesiology: the decline derived from a deteriorating capacity of the mainstream faithful actually to worship God; from a growing proclivity to cease from expecting church members to be disciples of Christ;

and from a corrupting emphasis on sentimentality and being "friendly" churches who then feel compelled to mask any truth that might smudge sentimental appearances.[7] I saw myself and my parishioners *choosing* to behave in ways that elicit indictments such as these.

My concern now is to employ a vocabulary that can convey the seriousness and the inescapability of choices (not choosing is a choice not to choose!) that testify to life as something that does not only *happen* to us. I know that modern existentialism has shared in the cultural solipsism that reduces truth to subjective attitude and will, an error exacerbated by the consequent existentialist attack on community in the name of individualistic choice. Existentialists often confused substantial truth with the personal commitment to it, reflecting an indifference to the content of truthfulness. But existential thought also affirmed—rightly I think—that something is not really true unless *action* is taken to realize it. And in my experience this affirmation is precisely what mainstream Protestants need to hear if they are to move beyond decay.[8]

More specifically, existentialists, especially Martin Heidegger, developed an analytic description of boredom that promises to elucidate the interior dimension of Protestant failure. They viewed boredom as a sign that a new stage of self-development or self-transcendence was pressing upon consciousness. If one chose to arrest growth and self-realization, then the bored condition mutated into threatening forms of apathy. Heidegger proposed that the human being could rise to become a Self with the ability to exercise consciously recognized choices (authenticity). Humans, however, usually operated in a state of "fallen-ness" (inauthenticity). In the latter respect, they anxiously fled—through distractions of busyness, chatter, and the like—the awareness of their responsibility for their own self-realization. Aiming to subordinate ethical evaluation to disinterested analysis, Heidegger sought merely to describe possible ways of being inauthentic, concluding that one of them occurred as the boredom that arose when people exercised choices inconsistent with their human *raison d'être* as self-realizing subjects. This inconsistency produced a kind of death, a killing of creative potential that manifested itself in apathy, indifference, ennui, depression, loss of vitality—boredom.[9]

Christians, whose *raison d'être* is the worship of God,[10] should understand that the existential analysis does have implications in the church for ethical action. Leander E. Keck argues that mainline Protestants have made their liturgical activity anthropocentric (evident, say, in weddings that arrange everything to demonstrate the primary importance of the *bride*), and hence have marginalized God, who "has become an amiable bore" while worship stales into "a memorial service to a fire gone out" (Keck 1993:36; see also n. 7 above). Keck's observations lead to the ethical judgment that mainstream churches have divorced themselves from their reason for being. Existential reasoning adds that unless they choose to act to renew their authenticity, these denominations will die of boredom.[11]

As indicated in the Introduction to this volume, I served as pastor of a mainline congregation far advanced toward this death. I do not believe adequate explanations for denominational decline will be found unless attention is concentrated on the frontline experiences of pastors. In the following material, therefore, I report my face-to-face encounter with the evidences of a congregation's boredom. I do not pretend that my experience in this particular church is generalizable in a scientific sense. Nor do I disclose identifying features of historical and sociological context that would enhance explanatory power by giving the congregation location. What I offer instead is something of a news bulletin that trumpets the bare facts of an event without providing contextual information. We might think of these data of experience as constituting an urgent message, a warning bulletin raising the possibility of a wider extremity. I believe I met a "boundary situation" significant for what it may of itself teach us regarding the mainstream Protestant malaise.[12] Pastors especially can compare their notes with mine and decide for themselves if I am reporting only an aberration.

The facts of the bulletin are itemized as follows:

- The congregation no longer upheld a working constitution and thus did not articulate covenant expectations for the membership.

- Religion had accordingly been reduced to the lowest common denominator; that is, each person could believe privately whatever he or she chose as long as no attempt was made to bind together with shared beliefs.

- The congregation had established a custom of allowing nonmembers to assume leadership positions in the church. (This practice aimed at "involving" the nonmember.)

- Not surprisingly, scarcely any spheres of responsibility and accountability were articulated parts of church government.

- Indeed, there was a multiyear pattern of fabricating the membership rolls.

- As a matter of course, with the exception of minimal expectations pertaining to premarital counseling, custodial matters, and user fees, congregational policy administered no religious, spiritual, or faith criteria regarding weddings, funerals, *or baptisms.* Upon request, each came automatically to the user.

- Leaders of the body viewed one of the primary strengths of the church as the "coffee and goodies time" that "builds fellowship."

- The congregation alternately made a variety of inter-pretations bearing on the above facts: constitutions represented legalism; covenant expectations would be "exclusive" and contrary to the spirit of openness and individual freedom; accurate membership rolls did not matter; shared norms of accountability would conflict with opinions privately held by individuals; being used for weddings, funerals, and baptisms was appropriate to the church's mission as a community "service" institution; and because God loved each person just as he or she was, it would be wrong for the church to tell anyone in the congregation how to think or behave.

- Congregational leadership simultaneously complained of widespread apathy toward the church. Apathy evinced in stagnant worship attendance, in the recy-cling of volunteers through boards, and the like. A recent pastor reputedly left "because he was bored." I was advised to expect little from worship and was told instead to "get involved in the community."

It obviously took many years and some peculiar contin-gencies to cook up conditions this extreme. It is equally obvious that most mainline congregations do not match with these circumstances. Yet perhaps the outermost odd-ity of this "boundary situation" discloses the inmost nature of the vacuum whose destructive vortex now moves from incipient stages to collapse a wider circumference of main-stream Protestant institutions. Whether this disclosure penetrates our consciousness depends on how we answer the bulletin.

Answering the Bulletin:
The Wages of "Pure Tolerance"

We might take the bulletin as a warning to be sensitive to a variety of things. It is possible to maintain that the congregation's plight should be addressed in therapeutic terms, viewing apathy as the result of a "discouraged" church needing to raise its self-esteem.[13] From another perspective, the situation may call for "long-range planning" that formulates a "strategic" intervention to improve accountability structures (see Callahan 1983:xv–xix, chap. 6). Or perhaps the congregation suffers from a "cycle of hopelessness" growing from years of spiritually diseased struggle to survive amid diminishing resources and promise (see Buttry 1988:chap. 1, esp. pp. 17, 21). Then again, it could be that environmental forces are undermining the church in a fashion beyond the control of the members.[14]

The bulletin notes ways in which the congregants answer for themselves. By turns they believe that constitutions equal legalism, disclaim the importance of accurate membership rolls, translate "inclusiveness" as privatization of beliefs, render Christian service as the satisfaction of civic demand for ceremonies, and claim that God's love makes congregational discipline unnecessary, to say nothing of being unjust. It could be added that all of these answers presume *passivity,* that is, passive tolerance of every opinion, every civic request, every convenient adjustment of the membership roster, and the like. To grapple, say, with the discipline requirements of constitutional order would mean an *active* assertion of identity, choosing to *be,* risking the displeasure of those who prefer a different identification. If we follow Kennon L. Callahan's reasoning, in *Effective Church Leadership,* when society establishes a "churched culture" that prompts people regularly to think of themselves as Christians and to be "seeking out" an available pew on Sunday morning, then a congregation can avoid self-identifying action and trust their destiny to the fact that the community wants citizens to participate in church functions. But when, as now, the conditions of disestablishment largely prevail, then on Sunday an "unchurched culture" makes many things appear more attractive than finding that pew. Callahan concludes that ecclesial practice fails when it stays inert in "maintenance" of what (facilities, programs, etc.) the culture once found interesting; it succeeds only as a "mission outpost" actively sharing the Christian faith (Callahan 1990:pt. 1, esp. pp. 10, 20, 23–25). Hence, disestablishment raises the imperative of existential action to live the Way. This venture will demand modification of a tolerance that cannot exercise disciplinary self-government, much less assume responsibility for extending mission in a world boding to become ungovernable.

Toleration requites our nonjudgmental attitude with acceptance from others. We all have foibles, and so we like this requital. On the other hand, should we place a limit on what we will tolerate? If so, which criteria will we use to settle on what this limitation will be? Herbert Marcuse evoked the thought that "pure" or indiscriminate tolerance—the conviction that no individual or group possesses truth sufficient to establish the governing boundaries of right and wrong—perforce means that all contending viewpoints cancel each other out. What remains? A nihilism grounded in defacto rule by powers that benefit from the status quo. There ensues the repression of attempts to alter this state of affairs, hence revealing the prior establishment of tolerance to have been spurious.[15] Wrestling with the implications of a similar toleration in mainline churches, Leander Keck indicates that a variety of Protestant interest groups compete and fail to affirm a shared truth, thereby ensuring that "something vital has been lost: the conviction that one *ought to be* a Christian." This belief might impede "mainliners' resolve to be open, inclusive, loving, affirming communities" who ironically suppress dissent by "implying that all opinions—from the bizarre to the banal—are welcome so long as they do not challenge the institution itself" (Keck 1993:116, 46).

Indiscriminate tolerance requites with its opposite—tyranny, loss of restraint on the exercise of power. Consider the example of the recent upheaval in the Southern Baptist denomination. "Moderates" in the body had long tried to handle dissension and to refrain from schism by anchoring Christian life in the "competency of the soul," whereby Spirit-led individuals enjoyed intimate relation to Jesus without the mediation of creed or ecclesiastical authority. Each individual was free to have direct experience with the Lord; so there should have been nothing (no creedal or other imposition) to fight over—except Moderate Southern Baptists also affirmed the authority of Scripture. But on what basis could they bind the denomination to this affirmation? They had already committed themselves to unlimited tolerance of individual experience as the final recourse for deciding what it meant to read the Bible. Sensing the vacuum of authoritative conviction, a virulent fundamentalism stepped into the cavity, seized denominational power, and vitiated tolerance itself. This pure toleration-authoritarian reaction pattern (symbiosis) points at once to loss of freedom on both sides of the dynamic, and to the inmost nature of current Protestant vacuity—the reduction of relationships to the exercise of power.[16]

If we might now return a discerning look at it, the warning bulletin also speaks from the vacuum about the wages of indiscriminate tolerance. A congregation that places nonmembers in leadership positions has no *Christian* idea where it is going; thence in tandem it must sacrifice *Christian* commitment to the lowest common denominator. When congregational policy routinely grants weddings, funerals, and baptisms, it also trivializes them by emptying them of *Christian* purpose. In a situation replete with such evidence of the lack of discipleship, it indeed may finally be appropriate, as I was advised, to expect little from worship. But the cost of this reduced expectation is the church's final loss of *Christian raison d'être*. In brief, apathy and ennui are fitting responses to a trivial, inauthentic institution that falls into nothingness. Like much of the rest of mainstream Protestantism, this congregation may persist in the Sunday-morning habits of "friendliness," believing that "coffee and goodies time" constructs the Faithful. Practices of sentimentality, however, cannot conceal the naked fact that the church's cornerstone is missing while the dry rot of boredom lays waste its foundation.

In sum, mainline Protestant denominations have experienced conditions of establishment (cultural expectations supporting ecclesial activity) giving way to those of disestablishment (reversal of the prior support), and Protestants find themselves needing to *act* to right their situation. Having historically fused with American culture, however, mainstream Protestantism is locked into a privatization of beliefs that spends itself in a toleration-reaction repetition that cannot extricate itself from the vacuum it signifies. Such extrication would mean, as Søren Kierkegaard testified in the not unrelated nineteenth-century context of Danish captivity of the church, that "official Christianity" would have to begin "frankly and unreservedly" to "make known the Christian requirement," to point out that Christ demanded radical loyalty over against "our own life in this world" (Kierkegaard 1868:38). Aside from tempting to the dangers of a stringent Christ-culture dualism,[17] this total allegiance would spell the end of privatized authority in the church. Yet the record of other Protestants would signal as well that this finish might be imperative.

4

Into the Vacuum:
The "Success" of "Evangelical" Marketing

It bears repeating that it might be taken as axiomatic that identifying (to the point of fusion) with an American culture in dissolution would bring trouble to churches who pursue this identification. Attend, though, to a classification-defying assortment of "evangelical" Protestants, who have much common sympathy for "born-again" experiences of spiritual renewal, but who then in broad terms range across a spectrum of "fundamentalists" distinguished by their doctrinal certitude (confidence, say, in the imminence of Christ's second coming) to pentecostals and charismatics who share experiential spirituality (divine healing and other gifts of the Holy Spirit) while refusing to be sharers of like denominational identity. These groups, as we will see below, generally fuse with the nation's cultural ideation and practice yet seem to be at the height of their success. Among evangelical denominations, the Assemblies of God recorded 71 percent membership gain during the period from 1973 to 1983. The Church of the Nazarene instanced a 22 percent increase over the same decade. Many evangelically inspired churches have remarkable stories to tell about how God has prospered them in the last thirty years. Nonetheless, again, we will explore the course set by our axiom.[1]

Whatever else evangelicals may or may not do, they do fuse with the American consumer marketplace. In the late 1980s, for example, if you attended the annual convention of the Christian Booksellers Association you encountered the expected efforts to bind, color, and translate Scripture so as to make it attractive in the multimillion-dollar Bible market. Although the sale of Bibles served as its mainstay, the assembly also featured "Personality Booths" where favorite evangelical musicians and writers handed out autographed issues of their works. The convention aimed as well to target cultural preoccupation with *techne* by selling books telling *How to Listen to God, How to Know You're Saved,* and *How to Be a Christian and Still Enjoy Life.* Salespersons meanwhile tendered "Christian" versions of punk rock, heavy metal, home videos, greeting cards, posters, T-shirts, sponges, combs, key chains, window decals, French provincial furniture, plush carpeting, and the ever-present bumper stickers (one of them reading: JESUS IS MY ROCK AND MY NAME IS ON THE ROLL). Such were some of the products annually retailed by Christian bookstores at the estimated sum of somewhere between $2 and $3.6 billion by the end of the 1980s.[2] William. B. Eerdmans' editor-in-chief, Jon Pott, examined the Association's rampant commercialism and noted, "I find it utterly demoralizing" (quoted in Balmer 1993:206).

The evangelical rush (dare it be called a *stampede?*) to consumer marketing takes monumental shape in "megachurches" that house religious programming after the fashion of shopping malls that offer specialty outlets catering to manifold tastes. Achieving Sunday attendance that varies from one to three thousand, these churches grow by effectively using "Church Growth" techniques stretching to include things like advertising developed through in-house congregant ad contests, and homogeneity cultivated as the governing criterion of congregational formation. (Institutions grow when they give people the comfort of affiliation with counterparts in the manner of customs; that is, like attracts like.) Exponents of growth encourage pastors and congregations to adopt the methods of efficient business. For example, George Barna, a leader among such promoters, argues that churches are caught in market-driven economic warfare and must appropriate techniques that capture marketplace niches (in other words, that secure adaptation to the "needs" of homogeneous groups). Barna reasons that in order to expand market share, congregations must enlarge to mega-size so that they can provide a range of programs to match with a variety of specialized group interests. Ecclesial practice, then, fails unless it discards the shackles of small-scale ambitions. Barna advocates the business corporation as the best model of what it means to be an *effective* church. In addition to Barna's fascination with the dimension of buying and selling, there is in the general evangelical fixation on marketing techniques a tendency determined so to blur the boundary between American marketeering and ecclesiastical objective that churches then confuse "success" with the purely quantitative terms of numerical increase.[3]

In their wholesale abolition of an identity distinct from the marketplace, evangelicals have submitted to market rule that conditions wants to parade as needs. Christian service becomes an effort to fulfill consumer needfulness, an exercise in nourishing subjective experience and producing the "good feelings" of customers satisfied with their religious choices. (Robert Schuller, for instance, can transmute the Sermon on the Mount from moral instructions to self-esteem tips for personal happiness.) Fulfillment of private desire becomes the standard by which church performance is measured. And this is the seedbed for troubling long-term results. Such privatization collapses Christian community restraints on full-scale marketing; thence "success" becomes merely a quantitative, material, mega-pursuit (a rather brutish quest when left to govern itself).

Ecclesial obsession fixes on techniques of power to succeed in marketplace warfare.[4] On the way to commercial
outcome, as David F. Wells apprehends, evangelical
expectations obliterate any conviction that gets in the
way of the search for private empowerment, a course that
bespeaks the church's capitulation to a cultural order
constituting "no system of belief at all. It is more like a
vacuum." In this emptiness instinctual satisfaction pre-
vails over ethical consideration and Wells finds himself
concentrating on the contemporary reality that "vacuums
may be empty, but they are highly destructive" (Wells
1993:169; and see also 87–92, esp. 92). Evangelicals,
then, might wish to remember that nineteenth-century
Americans had already discovered that unrestrained marketplace competition leads precisely to self-destruction.
No historical pattern is more certain than this operational
tendency of the "free" market.

Perhaps, though, if we listen to the stirring treatment of
pentecostal upsurge in Harvey Cox's *Fire from Heaven*, we
might detect in the mushroom advance of pentecostals the
possibilities of exodus from the moral vacuum of our age.
Cox here revises his 1960s projection that secularization
would make religion marginal and obsolete. His revision
isolates pentecostalism as a prime example of ours as "a
period of renewed religious vitality," a time of "another
'great awakening'... on a world scale." Pentecostal spirituality—"primal" experience of Spirit language like "speaking in tongues," of worship through body involvement in
acts of praise, and of eschatological vision that transcends
the dead end of marketplace materialism—promises to
generate energy that liberates people from the vortex of a
hollow culture. Moreover, when Cox points to pentecostalism's roots in racial reconciliation among the poor of Los
Angeles, a biblical parallel emerges, and it becomes
increasingly evident that the pentecostal phenomenon
cannot be dismissed prejudicially, a dismissal critics too

often issued in the past (see Cox 1995:xvi; see esp. chaps. 4–6, pp. xv, xvii, 104, 120–21, 315).

Sober words of caution, however, are in order. First, secularization is an ambiguous concept, and it is not clear that pentecostals pose any kind of substantial challenge to a secular order. That is, following the summary of secularization theories provided by Oliver Tschannen, we can see that secularizing forces usually restructure religion rather than eliminate it. There can be plural religious communities growing rapidly while also remaining privatized and partitioned off from the bureaucratic rationalization that governs society (see Tschannen 1994:70–72). Pentecostalism represents exactly the sort of experiential religion that readily lends itself to privatization. It is highly doubtful, then, that pentecostals form the advance wave of a new consensus for public (governing, civil religious, American) morality.

Second, in its fire of Spirit inspiration, spontaneity, and ecstatic fervor; in its propensity for attracting leaders who rise meteorically and fall self-destructively in the mold of tragic drama; in its striking capacity repeatedly to die and to rise, to renew after crashing onto the shoals of schism and other disorder—in all these respects pentecostalism appears to have more in common with Dionysian theater than with Christian faith.[5] (There is a vast difference between self-destructive excess and Christian martyrdom. The one dies for self, and the other dies for God and neighbor.)

Third, Cox draws a broad distinction between "fundamentalism"—the effort of any belief system to absolutize itself in an authoritarian fashion—and "experientialism"—the "personal" and pragmatic spirituality that is to religion what deregulation is to the economy—individualistic and anti-authoritarian. Cox views pentecostalism as "a battlefield" setting for these two impulses and fears that pentecostals will, in part, join the battle on terms that spell disintegration into "a vacuous 'cult of experience'" given to chaotic multiplication of self-absorbed interpretations of what it means to partake of "experience." We also recall from discussions above that this variety of duality is a quarrel between opposites who feed symbiotically on each other while resorting repetitively to imposition of power. This symbiosis traps its participants in the vortex of American cultural collapse.[6]

Fourth, as Cox observes, pentecostals in the United States seem especially prone both to forget their early development among the poor and to obscure the difference between Spirit vitality and the marketplace pomp that clamors "the-health-and-wealth gospel" of opulence for the deserving faithful (see Cox 1995:271–273, esp. 271). Fifth, a reading of *Fire from Heaven* discloses overbalanced pentecostal emphasis on the Spirit. This disproportion indicates a retreat from the Trinity and consequent failure to be Christocentric. Without the centrality of Christ, *Christ*ian self-understanding grows amorphous. Finally, for all these reasons, pentecostalism portends to become less a source of freedom from the contemporary vacuum and more a fountainhead of captivity to it.

In sum, the quantitative prosperity of evangelical denominations marks an adjustment to marketplace requirements that, on the one hand, shows how successfully evangelicals can adapt to the main currents of American culture while, on the other hand, masking evangelical deterioration into practice that cares ultimately for mega-success and the technicist power requisite for achieving it. Hence, in the wake of their passion to grow in size, evangelical churches increasingly dissipate Christian conviction as they fall into the moral vacuum that grows in cultural circumference. Pentecostalism represents a promising but highly questionable alternative to this dissipation. Pentecostals bid to spend themselves in Dionysian fervor, in lopsided experientialism that accents Spirit at the expense of the Christ who could constitute identity apart from the culture's "cult of experience." In a word, our axiom remains plausible: Fusion with American culture in dissolution brings trouble to churches who pursue this amalgamation. It will take something distinguishing to be the church.

5

Being the Church

The foregoing discussion prepared the ground for recognizing that the church in our day will get right by *doing* right by Jesus Christ. No reform gesture will be worth its salt unless it bespeaks resolution that is ethical and existential and not merely verbal; unless it *acts* resolutely to affirm distinctive Christian identity. Some readers may be prepared to charge me of Donatist and Pelagian fouls. This kind of existentialism seems in Chapter 3 above, for example, to make Christ's work in baptism dependent on the moral rigor and worth of the officiants (Donatism). In much of this volume, moreover, there appears to be the assumption that in ecclesial organizations human will can operate without inherent brokenness, and with a simple decision can choose either to follow the good example of Jesus or to chase the bad example of decadent culture (Pelagianism).[1] It cannot be stated too strongly, however, that we are caught in a cultural vortex that destroys the capacity for right action, that exhausts moral capital while plummeting into hopelessness.

This exhaustion is good news. It is not good because of what it will produce in history; untold suffering and sorrow await, and it is too late for human effort to steer an escape from these deplorable historical results. In the 1930s, in the wake of the Great Depression that witnessed to the darker possibilities of American development, H. Richard Niebuhr, in *The Church Against the World*, wrote from a context in which Protestantism despaired of a constructive role in the United States. He struck one of the many notes that characterized his aspiration to be a churchman willing to speak to the church's crisis. Niebuhr aided in articulating "the point of view of those who find themselves within a *threatened* church." Christians could never be fully in accord with the world, but there were periods when this abiding distinction seemed particularly pronounced. "We live," he explained, "in a time of hostility when the church is imperiled not only by an external worldliness but by one that has established itself within the Christian camp." Too many churches had "been on the retreat," had "made compromises with the enemy in thought, in organization, and in discipline." Amid this sea of halfway affirmations of faith, Niebuhr concluded that the sensible thing for the discerning church to do was to turn to the Lord and to hear "the command to halt, to remind itself of its mission, and to await further orders."[2] In our later time of cultural dissolution we can receive Niebuhr's words as a summons to stop, to realize our theoretical voluntarism, and to de-fuse our relationship with culture by canceling the organizational practices that reproduce the fusion—all so that we see ourselves and are seen by our neighbors as trusting God to regenerate and redirect us. During the stoppage—perhaps for a year?—we might only study the Bible, or we might simply pray. But deep down, repentance is what we will be living while stopped—to use that difficult word now resurrected by exponents of church renewal and meaning to undergo *metanoia* or complete change of ways.[3] So it is good news that America has exhausted its moral capital; connections to bad American habits will be broken, repenting can commence, and God's grace can start us over.

On the other side of repentance we will be ready to consider definite actions to be the church. Although many seem automatically averse to acknowledging its ongoing demise, one course of action will be closed—the effort to be influential in the shape of what William Stringfellow called "the Constantinian Arrangement" whereby Christians imbibe the "ethos" that stakes the church in supporting the dominant political regime (Stringfellow 1994:259, 260–261). One could extend Stringfellow's concept to include ecclesial backing for parties that aim in the name of reform to substitute one hegemonic rule with another. Theological argument against their propriety may not end either mode of Constantinianization, but history ultimately terminates Christian sensibilities and prerogatives in governing circles. Cultural disintegration now unfolds with an irreversible logic. If Christians try to continue in the Constantinian pattern, they will ineluctably take a desperate plunge into the vortex of that collapse. Sadly, there are scholars who perceive the symbiotic "bureaucratic individualism" that breaks a total way of life down to authoritarian recourse, yet even these intellectuals think that church proximity to political power can assist in a massive reformist solution to the breakdown, as if God especially favored such intimacy and such massiveness (cf., e.g., Bellah 1982:13–17, 19, 24, 26–27). Alasdair MacIntyre considers the scope of society's plight and doubts large-scale responses. How could these do other than rely on the very bureaucratization that requires solving? Moreover, as a practical matter, after the fall of socialism and in the midst of the decline of its social democratic surrogate, it becomes much harder for ecclesial advocates of "transformation" to hitch with a realistic politico-economic project to counter marketplace chaos.[4]

The church cannot be a sign of hope in a (historically, not ontologically) hopeless culture if Christians do not distinguish themselves from the hopelessness. The church, therefore, needs to be the "contrast-society" described by Gerhard Lohfink as Jesus' "city on the hill" whose reality as a visible countercommunity marks not an elitist retreat from the world but instead constitutes an invitation to live *for* the world by being an *identity* that in its difference discloses what others truly need (see Lohfink 1982:63ff.). To be sure, in ecclesiastical groups there is concern that the church not pursue its identity as an end in itself, that ecclesial focus not be restricted to internal affairs (cf. Messer 1992:17). It is well to heed the counsel of Douglas John Hall that "disengagement from the dominant culture" must be a dialectical moment in a process that leads the church beyond "abandonment" of the wider community to "authentic re-engagement of this same society" (Hall n.d.:14, 28, 15, see esp. 19). The reply to Hall is that concrete history makes *now* the time both to disengage and in basic ways to pursue the opposite of what the culture is doing.

The Church in Contrasts

Our ecclesial countersociety would operate safely within the boundaries established by the classic "marks of the church"—seeking to reconcile and unite with others, to show uncompromising ethics along with reverence for the holy, to be universally inclusive of everyone who confesses Christ, and to be a faithful messenger of the truth handed to the first apostles.[5] There is not the space here to rehearse these classical considerations; suffice to say that in our contemporary historical context it is important to accent those practices of Christian discipleship that break with the behaviors resulting from the vacuum unleashed by American culture. Distinct community is the embodiment of this departure, this renunciation of all theocratic temptations to locate God's agency foremost in a powerful state apparatus.[6]

Cruciform Christocentrism in contrast to power-centered nihilism

The church renounces theocratic pretensions to government dominion because its foundation is in the crucified One who made no claims to such aggrandizement. In keeping with the thought of Jürgen Moltmann, we affirm that the cross of Jesus needs to be seen retrospectively as the embodiment, the form, of the resurrection under the circumstances of human history. The risen Christ represents humanity and goes ahead of us into God's eschatological reign of righteousness and love, but this representation is representative precisely because it reaches back from the divine future into the human past of suffering and unrighteousness. The cross demonstrates the historical way of Easter hope as a method of vulnerability, self-sacrifice, nondomination, self-emptying, nonviolence; thus Golgotha serves simultaneously as the unique revelation of God's final destruction of evil, and hence the basis for Christian suffering both as a result of love for the world's despised and as an outcome of witness—sometimes expressed through martyrdom—against world rulers who arrogate ultimacy to themselves. The crucifixion, then, cannot be trumpeted in the manner of Constantinian triumphalism that adorns the throne of conquest with the cross; nor can this death be equated with cultic form that tries ritualistically to repeat Good Friday; nor can Golgotha's significance be restricted to interior mystical identification with the cross (see Moltmann 1991:53–65, 34, 43–44, 46, 50–52). We must instead arrange ourselves, as Arthur C. McGill intimated, as disciples for whom suffering is participation in Jesus' way of overcoming evil with crucified nonsuperiority. Such discipleship recognizes that when people "use force to exploit the weakness of others and by this means establish their superiority and domination over others, they are not then acting by the power of God." The practice of this power-to-be-superior is the opposite of cruciform humility and signals a procession belonging "to the realm of evil" (McGill 1982:86).

American culture exhausts itself through inability to believe that anyone possesses truthfulness sufficient to establish the governing boundaries of right and wrong. The resulting nihilism gives rise to Pilate's question: "What is truth?" (John 18:38a). But the church trusts that the true way—the authentic and righteous, the incorruptible and hopeful, the free and faithful path—is revealed in Jesus: "I am the way, and the truth, and the life. No one comes to the Father except through me" (John 14:6; cf. John 1:4; Eph. 4:21; 1 Cor. 3:11; Col. 2:9). Christians "must worship in spirit and truth" (John 4:24). That is, they should worship in the spirit of Jesus (John 5:33; 14:17; 15:26; 16:13). To be authentic, then, a Christian community will seek to center itself in Jesus. When it does this it becomes "the pillar and bulwark of the truth" (1 Tim. 3:15).[7]

The Christocentric church disobeys the rule of a nihilist culture. Contrary to cultural norm, it has a center, a reliable source of absolute truth grounding it as a countersociety given to cruciform humility. The culture refuses to absolutize any belief and ends up de facto absolutizing the coercive power that thrives in the absence of common standards of truthfulness. Countersociety Christians, on the other hand, proclaim absolutely the verity of Jesus and do so without fear of becoming overbearing. This fearless proclamation is possible because the absolute truth *is* cruciform.

Consider the example of the civil rights movement of the 1950s and 1960s. Under Martin Luther King, Jr.'s leadership, the movement's appeal stemmed from the practice of initiative and responsibility that eschewed claims of victimization that would have fueled self-righteous resentment in the oppressed and (an unyielding backlash of) guilt and hatred in the oppressor. Hence, the refusal to claim victim status helped the movement to avoid spending itself in cycles of retaliatory violence. This self-responsibility marked a concrete praxis of humility (I am no better than the other) and love (nonviolence as respect for the common brother/sisterhood of the other). Moreover, in the South where the movement experienced major successes, with these southern accomplishments later propelling favorable national legislation, it did so largely because of support from black churches, the strong local countersocieties that served as the backbone of the civil rights effort.[8] Bayard Rustin observed that the successful activism depended "upon the most stable institution of the southern negro community—the Church" (quoted in Lasch 1991:394). In the North, where this congregational foundation was not securely in place, the movement faltered in notable failures (exemplified by the ill-fated open-housing drive in Chicago) (see Lasch 1991:398–411).

It was not without consequence that King's leadership refused to collude with the duplicitous "Establishment" assumption that Christian faith could be a safe, nominal, comfortable experience. "We are gravely mistaken," King averred in 1967, "to think that religion protects us from the pain and agony of mortal existence. Life is not a euphoria of unalloyed comfort and untroubled ease… To be a Christian one must take up his cross" (quoted in Lasch 1991:392).

Interestingly, among Protestant clergy who supported the civil rights campaign, there was failure to learn some of the movement's central lessons. Instead of focusing, for instance, on the construction of local churches both strong in countersociety contrast and hence in capability of undergoing their cross, these clergy jumped ship and used much of their energy in reform activity apart from the task of leading their own congregations into re-formed Christian identity.[9] It has long since become crucial to reverse this error, to recover the charge to be distinctive, visible communions of Christ. It is time to repent from the mentality in the churches that seeks, as Lohfink describes it, to be so absorbed in reformist social transformation that in ecclesial terms it renounces "its own existence almost to the point of suicide." Indeed, "Is the idea that the church must immerse itself in the rest of society to the point of self-destruction really the right way to transform society?" (Lohfink 1982:64). It is now vital to answer this question with a good measure of indifference toward the competing political ideologies that would tempt with the promise of wielding some aspect of social dominion and thence confiscate the mental and emotional energy requisite for building local contrast-communities of Christians.[10] Suicidal immersion in reform activism is not the cruciform action that can change society first by manifesting the courage to be different from destructive societal expectations: Against the technicist obsession with prediction and control that rules America, countersociety Christians embrace a pentecostal awareness that the Holy Spirit, God's agency in perfecting creative historical possibilities, *will* "blow where it listeth" and will defy programs of political planning that panic at the prospect of spontaneity and in fear contravene God's surprising activity. The attendant point to the pentecostal emphasis is that practices must be judged to be of the Spirit only if they conform to the central criterion of cruciform discipleship. (The "health-and-wealth gospel" of acquisitiveness exemplifies failure to meet this standard.)[11]

In its visible conduct as a church, the Christocentric contrast-community will also counter the society's prevalent nihilism that issues specifically in a reasonless outlook. This attitude was forcefully expressed when a university student answered a reporter's query regarding possible American troop deployment in response to the Soviet Union's invasion of Afghanistan. The respondent insisted that, "There's nothing worth dying for" (quoted in Hauerwas and Willimon 1989:149). The Christian rejoinder to this declaration is that if there is *no* everlasting purpose for which to sacrifice life, then there is no reason beyond one-dimensional temporality for which to live life. The end is nothing. In the meantime, according to the saying, whoever acquires the most toys wins, and by implication whoever attains the most power gets the most toys. The end is power. And Christians reply that this chase after self-aggrandizement is a hopeless thing to live *and die* for. It is better to embrace the cross and to participate in Jesus' mission to show that God's future reign of love is here now in suffering and dying under the conditions of a world that does not know love. This embrace is a hopeful thing whose destiny is joy.[12]

Covenant in contrast to loss of Christian will

In biblical terms "covenant" signifies the way God rules, the means whereby the Sovereign made the gracious decision to enter a binding and intimate relationship with Israel. God commanded but did not coerce; Israel could choose to break the bonds of mutuality. This choice, however, incurred the consequences—historical calamities—of existence without God. The classic covenantal expression of God's commandments and Israel's obligations came through the mediation of Moses. Modern people must be careful not to construe covenant as equivalent to contemporary notions of "contract." The latter compact establishes a temporary bargain for the advancement of respective individual interests, whereas the former channels human will into the depth of long-range responsibilities of accountability and love that are necessary to sustain community.[13]

Christian tradition has tended to shape covenantal understanding in the pattern of God's unconditional promise of land for Abraham and his descendants (Gen. 15:18–21). Christians see in the covenant with Abraham a model of unmerited divine grace that prefigured God's gracious new covenant through Jesus Christ (see Gal.

4:21–28). Although it is true that Jesus' love liberates believers from the legalistic perfectionism that acts as if its own effort originated right relation to God, concurrently it is past time to admit that too many Christians have become flaccid in their reliance on a "forgiveness" that offers unconditionally to accept churchgoers even as it excuses them from serious commitment to Christian discipleship. To allude to the ever timely insight of Dietrich Bonhoeffer, "cheap grace" has become the reflex of Christians who want to *grant to themselves* an acceptance that allows them to be loved as they are. This "love" relishes the security of stasis and seeks to escape from God's freedom to judge and convict as moments in the holy love that spawns personal and communal transformation (see Bonhoeffer 1959:Pt. 1, esp. pp. 45–60).

Lest they challenge the sanctity of each individual's privately held "values," the churches retreat from disciplined affirmation of common beliefs (see, e.g., Johnson, Hoge, and Luidens 1993:13–18). Believe-as-you-wish individualism corrodes the very intention collectively to *be* Christians, deteriorates the capacity to be united *in Christ*—a routinization of corruption not unlike that described by the prophet Hosea as captivity of the will.[14] In my experience as a pastor, one of the last rationalizations encountered amid this slide into ethical deterioration is, "Jesus loves us even though we are not perfect." The response is, "Imperfection does not excuse infidelity to the Christian faith."

Our contemporary situation in the churches parallels that addressed by the Letter to the Hebrews. This letter testified that the covenantal promises made through the resurrection of Jesus surpassed those of any previous covenant (Heb. 3:5–6; 7:1–22; 8:8ff.; cf. Jer. 31:31–34). The author wrote, however, to people who jeopardized future assurances because of present flaccidity at once showing in "your drooping hands and... your weak knees" and betraying resolve to be "dull in understanding" (12:12; 5:11). This dullness produced ruination through failure to grasp that "the word of God is living and active, sharper than any two-edged sword, piercing until it divides soul from spirit, joints from marrow; it is able to judge the thoughts and intentions of the heart" (4:12).[15] Equally averse to indolent laxity, Jesus never annulled the sharp edge of Sinai covenant law. He summarized this sharpness in the commands to love God and neighbor (Matt. 22:34–40; Mark 12:28–34; Luke 10:25–28). Christians need again to hear that their authenticity, their *raison d'être,* resides in worship that obeys the first commandment: "You shall have no other gods before me" (Exod. 20:3).

Contemporary false gods of marketplace technique, individualist privatization, and the like, capture our praise and make us a cacophonous lot like those confronted by Paul in Corinth. The Corinthians communed not on the foundation of covenant in Christ, but on the basis of invidious distinctions of wealth or other status. Hence they made the Lord's Supper—that essential expression of Jesus' covenantal bond—into a meal that bespoke their dissolution of Christian identity (1 Cor. 11:20–22, 27). Instead of eating and drinking to participate in "the body of Christ," the Corinthians gathered to further their own self-importance and thus invited "condemnation" through self-destruction of the community (10:16; 11:34). Paul counseled them to remedy their situation by "discerning the body," by learning that their continuing communal disintegration evidenced the Lord's judgment that "disciplined" them to keep them from being "condemned along with the world" (11:29, 32).[16] There is no better counsel: We too must covenant to reassert the Christian will to initiate into this faith only those who desire seriously to *be* disciples of Jesus Christ.[17] The Lord's Supper will thereafter include everyone who chooses again and again to eat and drink and be full of no identity other than the one disclosed on the cross.

Practical Possibilities

The Christian contrast-society needs practical ways to get started with the task of enfleshing and embodying the life of discipleship. Possibilities for this embodiment are suggested below. These aim at nothing more than tentatively marking the kind of beginnings that ecclesiology will need to develop.

Cells

For a variety of reasons the cell-group church constitutes perhaps the best vehicle of ecclesial organization. First, from the vantage point of the Bible, home-based groups of between ten and twenty people appear to be entirely consistent with the ecclesiastical experience described in the Acts of the Apostles (see Shenk and Stutzman 1988:91–95). Second, from the perspective of our post-Constantinian age, the cells appropriately annul the anachronistic "Program Base Design" of the established territorial parishes of Christendom, thus canceling structures that enforce hierarchical and bureaucratic arrangement of committees that feed on specialized expertise while rendering many in the congregation passive and inactive (cf. Neighbour 1990:47 52). Third, from the point of view of sheer practical feasibility, cells would appear to be the best way to honor Max Weber's sage advice to those who want out of the twentieth century's organizational cage: "Only by reversion in every field—political, religious, economic, etc.—to small-scale organization would it be possible to any considerable extent to escape its [bureaucracy's] influence." (Weber 1947:338). Cells embody this "reversion" and afford the flesh-and-blood proximity whereby Christians know each other well enough to make covenant discipline meaningful as an expression of personal care. Cells allow this personalization, and so they contrast with large-scale organization's impersonal and hence destructive application of covenant in the form of abstract rules (cf. Neighbour 1990:chap. 5).

Cell groups are biblically and historically appropriate to matching the ecclesial challenge of a disestablished or post-Christendom society, but we must not employ them without paying critical attention to possibilities for their misguided (and dangerous) development. One can be permitted a nervous twitch or two when Ralph Neighbour, Jr., commences to unfold the elaborate structure of a cell group organization: Fifteen-person cells ("Shepherd groups") cluster to five cell churches guided by a "Zone Servant"; twenty-five groups with five Zone Servants cluster as a "congregation" under a "Zone Pastor"; and then twenty-five congregations with five Zone Pastors spell readiness for a truly massive "celebration" of the total cell body. The "Senior Pastor Ministry Team" provides overall direction. There is throughout this structure an apparent reliance upon the "truly *anointed* leader." Or, as another example, consider the African cell church launched by Dion Robert: Cell-based departments—for family life, evangelism, demonology, missionaries, publications, administration—develop along a pattern that seems to replicate the bureaucratic design of the business corporation; that is, centralized direction of functionally fragmented offices. What is to prevent a similar replication from occurring in the shepherd-zone system? What is to stop the "anointed leader" from becoming a centralized bureau-technocrat? Can we defeat bureaucracy by governing ourselves bureaucratically? One is almost prepared to embrace the methodology of the "House Church" that refuses to extend structure outside the house (except that this method curtails mission outreach). What is to be done?[18]

On the one hand, the Scylla of decentralization (exemplified by the home-bound house churches) produces fear of expansion and consequent disconnection from the unity and mission of the larger Christian body. On the other hand, the Charybdis of missionary expansion brings the threat of centralization and reintroduction into the church of the "iron cage" of large-scale organization and practices. The greater menace, however, arises from using cells as the foundation for empire building and mega-formation. This use fails the test of a cruciform church whose humble practice recognizes both that there are "no large remedies" for late twentieth-century problems, and that there will be much reproduction of bureaucratization resulting from belief in such solutions.

Spiritual disciplines

In my pastoral experience I have found the work of Richard J. Foster and Dallas Willard on spiritual disciplines (prayer, fasting, study, service, simplicity, worship, and the like) to be a helpful way to introduce Christians to the awareness that discipleship is an ongoing, daily, practical incarnation of the spirituality demonstrated by Jesus in regular conduct. In this context of discipleship, "discipline" relinquishes the connotation of punishment and assumes that of training or preparation for the times of challenge and grace that await. Considering the historical nightmare developing in the West, it is now essential to prepare for the likelihood that martyrdom will become in many instances the only way to remain faithful.[19]

6

Summary and Conclusion

The seventeenth- and eighteenth-century Enlightenment overthrew the traditional authority of moral claims grounded in Christian and Aristotelian teleology. Unable to establish rational or supratraditional standards of morality in the wake of this overthrow, the Enlightenment resulted in a split of the Western world: on the one hand, into the realm of public "facts," and, on the other hand, into the domain of private "values." Nineteenth-century agrarian Populism represented the last realistic American opportunity to mend this tear in the name of a common biblical-*cum*-republican morality. The defeat of Populism in 1896 removed impediments to the transfer of government from moral terms to those of the amoral rule of efficient expertise and bureaucratic management. American history marks an intensifying symbiosis joining cultural disintegration of ethical consensus with consequent reliance on bureaucracy for the maintenance of order. This dissolution combined with bureaucratization to widen the vortex of a moral vacuum that increasingly prospers the unrestrained exercise of power and violence.

"Mainline" Protestants watched as their "cultural establishment" (like-minded church-nation reciprocity) gave

way to individualist privatization of religious beliefs, an
expression of privacy that mainliners embraced and then
followed into a vacuum where they tried to tolerate all
viewpoints indiscriminately and ended up with intoler-
ance. "Evangelical" Protestants, meanwhile, so "successfully" adapted to marketplace norms that they accelerated
collapse of restraint on pursuit of the power requisite for
winning in the market. To do right by Jesus Christ, many
Christians in America must undergo *metanoia*—a complete change of ways—and then assert a distinctive identity
that is at once cruciform and covenantal.

In a volume entitled *Crossing the Postmodern Divide*,
Albert Borgmann searches for a "postmodern realism"
whose attentive, patient, gentle, celebratory spirit can
surpass the wreckage that unfolds both from a "modern
project" of aggression against nature and from a technology-
facilitated "hypermodernism" that elevates restless and
disoriented speed to a virtue. Borgmann raises hope that a
genuine celebration of cooperation, a true postmodern
"heavenly city," can succeed in church and in the American
nation (see Borgmann 1992:esp. 5–6, 12–19, 143–147). I
believe in this age that it can be successful in the *church,*
and I believe this because I believe the promise: "And I tell
you, you are Peter, and on this rock I will build my church,
and the gates of Hades will not prevail against it" (Matt.
16:18). Now is the time to trust that God can raise up a
cruciform people. Nothing can defeat the resurrection of
Jesus Christ; not even barbarism! Praise the Lord!
Hallelujah!

Notes

Introduction

1. In this volume I have elected to withhold both the name of the denomination and the identities of the congregations that provided the environment for my pastoral experience.

2. Paul's adaptation of the image of the body is discussed in Betz and Mitchell 1992:1:1147.

3. The following discussion of the Enlightenment is based on MacIntyre 1984:chaps. 1–9, esp. pp. 44–46, 52–56, 117.

4. Cf. this understanding of Christian *telos* with Harvey 1964:141–142.

5. Discussion of courage is in Tillich 1952:esp. 1–3, 172–188. The dialectical movement is treated in Tillich 1963:284; and Tillich 1951:234–235.

6. The reason for quotation marks around "mainline" and "decline" is indicated in Chapter 3.

7. The reason for quotation marks around "evangelical" is indicated in Chapter 4.

Chapter 1: Vignettes from the Vacuum: Pastoral Ministry amid the Collapse of Church Identity

1. Cf. with Hauerwas 1991:15–16. Cf. these questions with Hauerwas and Willimon 1989:149.

2. Cf. these questions with Hauerwas and Willimon 1989:149.

Chapter 2: The Symbiosis of Bureaucracy and
Cultural Disintegration: Entering the Age of Barbarism

1. Indiana Republican Congressman quoted in Foner 1970:39.

2. On the ideals of independence and the Homestead Act, see Shannon 1945:52; Smith 1950: chap.15; and Hofstadter 1955:23–36. On the aspirations of Protestantism, note the exploration of the array of agencies that advanced a protestant *"paideia,"* in Cremin 1980:chap. 11, 311–318. Aspects of character receive description in Wyllie 1954:chap. 3, 22–23.

3. On the American use of Locke, see Hartz 1955:60–61.

4. Antebellum data are from Foner 1970:31–33; the "Go-Getters" are described in Boorstin 1973:3–4, 49–52, esp. 49.

5. Good discussions of the import of efforts of industrialization and settlement are in Higgs 1971:80–81; and Boorstin 1973:120–121.

6. The topics in this paragraph are addressed in Bellah 1992:chaps. 1–3, esp. pp. 12–35, 81.

7. For observations on the growth of factories, see Wiebe 1967:20–21; and Rodgers 1978:24–25. Note particularly the impact of the railroad on agriculture in Cochrane 1979:201–202, 220.

8. General incorporation laws and formation of combinations of corporations are dealt with in Boorstin 1973:414–419; and a good discussion of corporate integration is in Porter 1973:43–71, 89-90. Distinction between horizontal experiments is drawn by Wiebe 1967:24n.

9. Speaking before the U.S. Industrial Commission (1898–1901) and quoted in Porter 1973:89–90.

10. On the extent of corporate corruption, see Ginger 1965:33–34; and Zinn 1980: 248–251. The Sherman Act is treated in Hofstadter 1955:233.

11. See Bellah 1992:25–27, for helpful reflection on Hobbes. On the markets, see Ginger 1965:157–159. Business

failures and unemployment figures are recorded in Zinn 1980:271–272; and the path of farm prices is available in Cochrane 1979:93–95.

12. Data on working conditions are noted in Pelling 1960:81; strike details are in Brecher 1972:31, 53–63, 69, 78–96.

13. Wiebe 1967:35–36, 91–94 discusses late nineteenth-century presidential behavior; and Brecher 1972:63–78, 85–89 details the use of force to break strikes.

14. On the origin of Populism and the Alliance's break from the practice of confining cooperative buying and selling to relatively advantaged strata, see Goodwyn 1976:chap. 7, 120 121, 138–139.

15. The initiation of the Alliance and number and spread of suballiances are detailed in Goodwyn 1976:25, 33–40, 86, 122. It should be noted, however, that the suballiances—the basic local units of the National Alliance—contained teachers, preachers, and others besides farmers. See Dyson 1986:201.

16. For extended commentary on the subjects raised in this paragraph, see Lasch 1991:217–225.

17. On producers versus speculators, see Foner 1970:11–12, 19–20; and cf. Lasch 1991:222.

18. Descriptions of Populism and Davis quoted in Goodwyn 1976:194, 373.

19. Regarding the tension in Populism, see n. 34 below; Zinn 1980:255 addresses the Supreme Court's understanding of both the business corporation and the Fourteenth Amendment.

20. The emergence and substance of the Omaha Platform are treated at length in Goodwyn 1976:230, 264–267, 270–272; and Palmer 1980:69–125 passim. Populists contended that valid relations to land involved the use of it, not the speculative trading of it.

21. Lasch 1965:88 notes that "cooperative common-wealth" was a designation with currency among many American reform groups. In particular, Green 1980:19, 21–22 explains that Socialists associated it with cooperative control of the means of production, but Populists usually limited its applicability to the means of distribution.

22. Palmer 1980:chap. 4, pp. 31–32, discusses Lockian principles in Populism; and Goodwyn 1976:chaps. 8, 13–16, pp. 142–172 passim, details the tear in Populism, the opposition of businessmen, and the decline resulting from reliance on the silver issue.

23. Regarding these constraints, cf. the observation by Palmer (1980:24), noting "the Southern Populists' commitment to a Christianity which measured public as well as private morality."

24. Quotations in the paragraph are in Goodwyn 1976:265, 354, 381.

25. On the defeat of the reformers, see Goodwyn 1976:492 493.

26. Goodwyn 1976:540; see also 537 for twentieth-century implications of the decline of farmers' Populism.

27. McCormick 1981:259–274 addresses the impact of the moral rhetoric of muckrakers. On corporate consolidation: Figures for 1897 to 1903 are from Cochran 1957:58–59. The estimate for 1895 to 1905 is in Porter 1973:78. For 1919 data, see Faulkner 1961:155. Regarding the centralizing impact of regulatory activity, see Sklar 1988: 36–39, 325, 334–363, 420–421.

28. On the meanings of efficiency, see Haber 1964. Berman 1981:41–45; and White 1968:11, 20, 77, 79 address ramifications of Newtonian and Western conceptions. The derivation of competence from university training is observed in Bledstein 1976:105–120.

29. Quoted in Hays 1980:104, 124, see also chap. 3, pp. 271–272, 275, for discussion of the nature of the conservation movement.

30. Regarding improvement and acquiring more, cf. Lasch 1991:47–48.

31. On this constitution of Populism, cf. Goodwyn 1976:537.

32. On the subjects in the last two paragraphs, see MacIntyre 1984:35, 34, 68.

33. Regarding matters of civil religion, see Bellah 1992:164–178, esp. 166, 177–178.

34. Quotations in this paragraph are in Wuthnow 1988:38, 45, 43; see also 44, 52, 40, for discussion of other points in the paragraph.

35. Quotations in this paragraph are in Wuthnow 1988:36, 49; and see also 35–37, 50, for other facts mentioned in this paragraph.

36. Quoted in Wuthnow 1988:57, see also 66 for mention of Morse.

37. On the divisions of the 1960s and plural faith developments, see Wuthnow 1988:142–152, esp.148; and Hunter 1991:73–76, 86–95, esp. 88.

38. On the themes of culture war that are discussed in this paragraph, cf. Hunter 1991:passim, esp.43; and on grabbing fragments, see MacIntyre 1984:1–5.

39. Hunter 1991:131; see also 119–130, esp. 120–125, for discussion of incompatible foundations of moral authority.

40. To this point in this paragraph, cf. Hunter 1991:pt. 4.

41. American Family Association advertisement quoted in Hunter 1991:231.

42. Regarding defenders of the artists and upholders of community standards, see Hunter 1991:232, 238, 247; MacIntyre 1984:66–70 suggests the query respecting why the "right" should be honored. Pertaining to the will to power, see Nietzsche 1901:35–39.

43. On the fragile foundation of American order, cf. Carter 1993:chap. 2, esp. p. 25.

44. Davis 1994:passim, esp. 121, describes a general process whereby the veterans got caught in a situation that shattered American confidence that everything could be controlled through application of scientific technique. Soldiers had imbibed this trust and then experienced its destruction during the conflict. In connection with the control/measure mentality that was at work in Vietnam, it is constructive to see the admission in McNamara 1995:323 that during the war, "We failed to recognize that in international affairs, as in other aspects of life, there may be problems for which there are no immediate solutions. For one whose life has been dedicated to the belief and practice of problem solving, this is particularly

hard to admit. But, at times, we may have to live with an imperfect, untidy world."

45. On bureaucratic rationalization, see Weber 1947:esp. 329–340. An incisive summary of Weber's thought is Lurkings 1975:18.

46. On the structure of Western societies as an environment of techniques, see Ellul 1964:xxv–xxvi; and Ellul 1989:chap. 11. Ellul 1967:146 treats the bureaucratic manifestation of technicism. A very helpful summary of Ellul's understanding of the relationship between means and ends in a technological society is Holloway 1970:7.

47. Individualism and positive thinking are observed in Stivers 1994:24–25, 64–65; and Bellah 1985:120, 221–224.

48. On consumption of lifestyle and vicarious drama, cf. Stivers 1994:chaps. 3, 6; and for interesting suggestions regarding psychotherapy's compensation, see Mills 1976:295. The lack of challenge to the presuppositions of social organization is noted in Bellah 1985:224.

49. Stivers 1994:23, 90–91 refers to James and observes the tendency toward cynicism.

50. In this regard, see the interesting reflections on the need for "de-theorization" of the technicism that "renders opaque" both the possibility of creative human action and hence the capacity to be ethical, in Fashing 1980:154–156.

51. Crenshaw 1992:2:271–272, 275–277 informs the understanding of Ecclesiastes in the discussion below; the interpretation of Qoheleth's wisdom is primarily dependent on Ellul 1990:esp.281–283.

52. The interpretation of Ecclesiastes in this paragraph is shaped by Ellul 1990:esp. 281–283; and see also n. 51 above.

53. Newbigin 1995:27, and see also 23, 51–52, 76, 83, for matters related to postmodern criticism.

Chapter 3: Into the Vacuum:
Disestablishment and "Mainline" Protestant Failure

1. Regarding what merits "mainline" classification, see Coalter, Mulder, and Weeks 1992:1–14; and Keck 1993:20. On

membership decline and defensive arguing, see Coalter, Mulder, and Weeks 1990:17, 19, 27; and Keck 1993:19, 21–22.

2. The issues to this point in the paragraph are discussed in Wright 1984:178–179.

3. The incorporation of voluntary associations is treated in Weeks 1991:101–109; Luidens 1982:163–175 provides an example regarding the subject of centralized ecclesiastical power. On "Christ of culture," see the classic study by Niebuhr 1951:chap. 3.

4. On the "cultural establishment" of Christianity, see Hall n.d.:6–8.

5. The substantial losses are noted in Hall 1989:50–51; Carroll and Roof 1993:12–13 observe the data since the 1960s.

6. On the final unraveling of the Constantinian-Theodosian Establishment, see Hall 1989:28–30, 50–51.

7. For conclusions of contemporary ecclesiology, see Keck 1993:34–38 on the decline of the worship of God; Willard 1988:258–265 on ceasing from discipleship; and Hauerwas and Willimon 1989:120, 138 on sentimentality.

8. Regarding errors of existentialism, see Shinn 1968:53, 80–82, 84–86; and for right affirmations of existentialism, see Shinn 1968:11–22.

9. On the nature of boredom and the existential perception of human action, see Schrader 1967:26–28; Barrett 1958:chap. 9; and Molina 1962:chap. 4.

10. See the Introduction to this volume.

11. In a related context, Hauerwas and Willimon 1989:122 remark, "If the laity are not serious about their own ministry, not continually raising the questions which faithful living in the world demands, then they will get pastors who seem to have forgotten God's story. Church will be a source of conventional, socially acceptable answers, a place to reiterate what everybody already knows, even without the church. *We shall die, not from crucifixion, but from sheer boredom*" [emphasis mine].

12. A concept given currency by Karl Jaspers and Paul Tillich, "boundary situations" are defining realities of human existence that confront people with the possibility of making

authentic decisions. Such realities are death, conflict, and the like. See Harvey 1964:45. As can be seen below, in the parish in question I encountered a way of dying.

13. This is an important theme in Swan 1990:89–107 passim.

14. Unfavorable demographics is a common resort (and source of comfort) for those who believe that decline is outside their control. See Coalter, Mulder, and Weeks 1992:247.

15. See the many-sided argument developed in the classic critique by Marcuse 1969:81–123, esp. 85, 88–91, 92n, 94–97.

16. On the Southern Baptist upheaval, see Bloom 1992:chaps. 13–14; and for an alternative appraisal, see Leonard 1993:905–910.

17. Consider, for example, the import of the strict dichotomy between churches that resist and those that accommodate secularization, in Gilbert 1980:esp. 153.

Chapter 4: Into the Vacuum:
The "Success" of "Evangelical" Marketing

1. On the assortment of evangelicals, see Balmer 1993:xiii–xvi. The numerical data are in Wells 1994:22n. For a classic perspective on evangelical prosperity, see Kelley 1972.

2. On the Christian Booksellers convention, see Balmer 1993:chap. 10, esp. pp. 199 200, 203.

3. Regarding the subjects discussed in this paragraph, see Wells 1994:60–82.

4. For discussion of privatization and Schuller, see Wells 1993:72–74, 168–186, esp. 175; and on pursuit of power in the marketplace, see Wells 1994:74, 79–80, 82, 84, 153.

5. For characteristics of pentecostalism, see Cox 1995:150–155, 279, 77–78; and on the nature of Dionysian theater, see Hamilton 1969:60–62.

6. Regarding pentecostalism as a battlefield for the dual impulses, see Cox 1995:esp. 300, 306, 310, 313.

Chapter 5: Being the Church

1. On Donatism and Pelagianism, see Brauer 1971:275, 644–645.

2. Niebuhr 1935:1, 2; regarding Niebuhr's churchman aspirations, see Frei 1957:12n.

3. Exponents calling for repentance are Coalter, Mulder, and Weeks 1992:246–247; and Keck 1993:25.

4. On the church's relation to such a project, cf. Newbigin 1994:196–197.

5. Cf. with the perception of these marks in Hall 1989:88–103.

6. On renunciation of theocracy, cf. Lohfink 1982:72.

7. Regarding the Christocentrism presented in this paragraph, see also McKenzie 1965:901–902.

8. In the discussion here and below, both the mention of facts pertaining to the civil rights movement and the interpretation of the campaign are dependent on Christopher Lasch 1991:393–398.

9. For observation on the reform activity of Protestant clergy, see Lasch 1991:410.

10. Note the implications of this indifference in the discussion of the dichotomy between theology and politics in Eller 1987:esp. p. 2, chap. 7. It seems to me that, in part, Ellul 1988:12–23, moderates the dichotomy, implicitly transforming it into a dialectic.

11. On the Holy Spirit as God's perfecting agency, see Rosato 1983:262; and for pentecostal and "health-and-wealth" emphases, see Cox 1995:151, 271–273.

12. Regarding the eschatological significance of the cross, see Moltmann 1974:178–187, 55–56.

13. The nature of covenant is discussed in Mendenhall and Herion 1992:1:1180–1187; modern versus biblical understandings are in Elazar 1980:3–30.

14. See the discussion of Hosea in Ward 1991:228.

15. On Hebrews, see also Johnson 1986:414–415, 419.

16. Regarding Paul's counsel, see also Johnson 1986:286.

17. Concerning serious initiation into the Christian faith, see the mentor-based approach to confirmation in Willimon 1990.

18. On the shepherd-zone system and Robert's effort, see Neighbour 1990:chaps. 13, 25, esp. pp. 194–196, 207, 203; the

bureaucratic design of the business corporation is described in Chandler 1977:6–12.

19. On disciplines as training, see Foster 1988:esp. 1–11. For local congregations interested in practicing the disciplines, it is important to use Foster 1983; on the disciplines as incarnating the spirituality demonstrated by Jesus, see Willard 1988: chaps. 1, 9.

References Cited

Allen, Ronald J. 1994. "The Disciples: A Denomination in Code Blue." *The Disciple*, Jan., pp.16–17.

Balmer, Randall. 1993. *Mine Eyes Have Seen the Glory: A Journey into the Evangelical Subculture in America.* New York: Oxford University Press. Expanded ed.

Barrett, David B., ed., 1982. *The World Christian Encyclopedia.* Nairobi: Oxford University Press.

Barrett, William. 1958. *Irrational Man: A Study in Existential Philosophy.* Garden City: Doubleday Anchor Books.

Bellah, Robert N. 1982. "Discerning Old and New Imperatives in Theological Education." *Theological Education* 19 (Autumn):13–17, 19, 24, 26–27.

———. 1992. *The Broken Covenant: American Civil Religion in Time of Trial.* Chicago: University of Chicago Press. 2d ed.

Bellah, Robert N., et al. 1985. *Habits of the Heart: Individualism and Commitment in American Life.* New York: Harper & Row, Perennial Library.

Berman, Morris. 1981. *The Reenchantment of the World.* Ithaca: Cornell University Press.

Betz, Hans Dieter, and Margaret M. Mitchell. 1992. "Corinthians, First Epistle to The." In *The Anchor Bible Dictionary.* Ed. David Noel Freedman et al. 6 vols. New York: Doubleday & Co.

Bledstein, Burton J. 1976. *The Culture of Professionalism: The Middle Class and the Development of Higher Education in America.* New York: W. W. Norton.

Bloom, Harold. 1992. *The American Religion: The Emergence of the Post-Christian Nation.* New York: Simon & Schuster, Touchstone.

Bonhoeffer, Dietrich. 1959. *The Cost of Discipleship.* New York: Macmillan, Collier. Rev. ed.

Boorstin, Daniel J. 1973. *The Americans: The Democratic Experience.* New York: Vintage Books.

Borgmann, Albert. 1992. *Crossing the Postmodern Divide.* Chicago: University of Chicago Press.

Brauer, Jerald C., et al., eds. 1971. *The Westminster Dictionary of Church History.* Philadelphia: Westminster Press.

Brecher, Jeremy. 1972. *Strike!* Boston: South End Press.

Buttry, Daniel. 1988. *Bringing Your Church Back to Life: Beyond Survival Mentality.* Valley Forge: Judson Press.

Callahan, Kennon L. 1983. *Twelve Keys to an Effective Church: Strategic Planning for Mission.* San Francisco: HarperCollins.

———. 1990. *Effective Church Leadership: Building on the Twelve Keys.* San Francisco: HarperCollins.

Carroll, Jackson W., and Wade Clark Roof. 1993. "Introduction." In *Beyond Establishment: Protestant Identity in a Post-Protestant Age.* Ed. Carroll and Roof. Louisville: Westminster/John Knox Press. Pp. 11–27.

Carter, Stephen L. 1993. *The Culture of Disbelief: How American Law and Politics Trivialize Religious Devotion.* New York: HarperCollins, Basic Books.

Chandler, Alfred D., Jr. 1977. *The Visible Hand: The Managerial Revolution in American Business.* Cambridge: Harvard University Press, Belknap.

Coalter, Milton J., John M. Mulder, and Louis B. Weeks. 1990. "Introduction." In *The Mainstream Protestant "Decline": The Presbyterian Pattern.* Ed. Coalter, Mulder, and Weeks. Louisville: Westminster/John Knox Press. Pp. 17–28.

———. 1992. *The Re-Forming Tradition: Presbyterians and Mainstream Protestantism.* Louisville: Westminster/John Knox Press.

Cochran, Thomas C. 1957. *The American Business System: A Historical Perspective, 1900–1955.* New York: Harper Torchbooks.

Cochrane, Willard W. 1979. *The Development of American Agriculture: A Historical Analysis.* Minneapolis: University of Minnesota Press.

Cox, Harvey. 1995. *Fire from Heaven: The Rise of Pentecostal Spirituality and the Reshaping of Religion in the Twenty-first Century.* Reading, Mass.: Addison-Wesley.

Cremin, Lawrence A. 1980. *American Education: The National Experience, 1783–1876.* New York: Harper Colophon.

Crenshaw, James L. 1992. "Ecclesiastes, Book of." In *The Anchor Bible Dictionary.* Ed. David Noel Freedman et al. 6 vols. New York: Doubleday & Co.

Davis, Jr., Walter T. 1994. *Shattered Dream: America's Search for Its Soul.* Valley Forge: Trinity Press International.

Descartes, René. 1951. *A Discourse on Method and Selected Writings.* Trans. John Veitch. New York: E. P. Dutton.

Dyson, Lowell K. 1986. *Farmers' Organizations.* New York: Greenwood.

Elazar, Daniel J. 1980. "The Political Theory of Covenant: Biblical Origins and Modern Developments." In *Covenant, Polity, and Constitutionalism.* Ed. Elazar and John Kincaid. Lanham: University Press of America. Pp. 3–30.

Eller, Vernard. 1987. *Christian Anarchy: Jesus' Primacy over the Powers.* Grand Rapids: Eerdmans.

Ellmann, Richard. 1948. *Yeats: The Man and the Masks.* New York: E. P. Dutton.

Ellul, Jacques. 1964. *The Technological Society.* Trans. John Wilkinson. Introd. Robert K. Merton. New York: Vintage Books.

———. 1967. *The Political Illusion.* Trans. Konrad Kellen. New York: Vintage Books.

———. 1988. *Anarchy and Christianity.* Trans. Geoffrey W. Bromiley. Grand Rapids: Eerdmans.

———. 1989. *What I Believe.* Trans. Geoffrey W. Bromiley. Grand Rapids: Eerdmans.

———. 1990. *Reason for Being: A Meditation on Ecclesiastes.* Trans. Joyce Main Hanks. Grand Rapids: Eerdmans.

Fashing, Darrell J. 1980. "Technology as Utopian Technique of the Human." *Soundings* 63 (Summer 1980):154–156.

Faulkner, Harold U. 1961. *The Decline of Laissez-Faire.* New York: Holt, Rinehart and Winston.

Foner, Eric. 1970. *Free Soil, Free Labor, Free Men: The Ideology of the Republican Party Before the Civil War.* New York: Oxford University Press.

Foster, Richard J. 1983. *Richard J. Foster's Study Guide for Celebration of Discipline.* San Francisco: Harper & Row.

———. 1988. *Celebration of Discipline: The Path to Spiritual Growth.* San Francisco: Harper & Row. Rev. ed.

Frei, Hans W. 1957. "Niebuhr's Theological Background." *In Faith and Ethics: The Theology of H. Richard Niebuhr.* Ed. Paul Ramsey. New York: Harper Torchbooks.

Gilbert, Alan D. 1980. *The Making of Post-Christian Britain: A History of the Secularization of Modern Society.* London: Longman.

Ginger, Ray. 1965. *Age of Excess: The United States from 1877 to 1914.* New York: Macmillan.

Goodwyn, Lawrence. 1976. *Democratic Promise: The Populist Moment in America.* New York: Oxford University Press.

Green, James. 1980. "Populism, Socialism, and the Promise of Democracy." *Radical History Review* 24 (Fall):19, 21, 22.

Haber, Samuel. 1964. *Efficiency and Uplift: Scientific Management in the Progressive Era, 1890–1920.* Chicago: University of Chicago Press.

Hall, Douglas John. 1989. *The Future of the Church: Where Are We Headed?* N.p.: United Church Publishing House.

———. N.d. *An Awkward Church.* Theology and Worship Occasional Paper No. 5. Louisville: Presbyterian Church U.S.A.

Hamilton, Edith. 1969. *Mythology*. Illus. Steele Savage. New York: New American Library. First published 1940.

Hartz, Louis. 1955. *The Liberal Tradition in America: An Interpretation of American Political Thought Since the Revolution*. New York: Harcourt Brace Jovanovich.

Harvey, Van A. 1964. *A Handbook of Theological Terms*. New York: Macmillan.

Hauerwas, Stanley. 1991. *After Christendom? How the Church Is to Behave If Freedom, Justice, and a Christian Nation Are Bad Ideas*. Nashville: Abingdon Press.

Hauerwas, Stanley, and William H. Willimon. 1989. *Resident Aliens: Life in the Christian Colony*. Nashville: Abingdon Press.

Hays, Samuel P. 1980. *Conservation and the Gospel of Efficiency: The Progressive Conservation Movement, 1890–1920*. New York: Atheneum. First published 1959.

Higgs, Robert. 1971. *The Transformation of the American Economy, 1865–1914: An Essay in Interpretation*. New York: Wiley.

Hofstadter, Richard. 1955. *The Age of Reform: From Bryan to F.D.R.* New York: Vintage Books.

Holloway, James Y. 1970. "West of Eden." *Katallagete* 2 (Winter/Spring):7.

Hunter, James Davison. 1991. *Culture Wars: The Struggle to Define America*. New York: HarperCollins, Basic Books.

Johnson, Benton, Dean R. Hoge, and Donald A. Luidens. 1993. "Mainline Churches: The Real Reason for Decline." *First Things* 31 (March):13–18.

Johnson, Luke Timothy. 1986. *The Writings of the New Testament: An Interpretation*. Philadelphia: Fortress Press.

Keck, Leander E. 1993. *The Church Confident*. Nashville: Abingdon Press.

Kelley, Dean. 1972. *Why Conservative Churches Are Growing*. New York: Harper & Row.

Kierkegaard, Søren. 1968. *Attack upon "Christendom."* Trans. and Introd. Walter Lowrie. Princeton: Princeton University Press. Danish orig. 1854–55.

Lasch, Christopher. 1965. *The New Radicalism in America, 1889–1963: The Intellectual as a Social Type.* New York: Vintage Books.

——. 1991. *The True and Only Heaven: Progress and Its Critics.* New York: W. W. Norton.

Leonard, Bill J. 1993. "When the Denominational Center Doesn't Hold: The Southern Baptist Experience." *The Christian Century* 22–29 (September.):905–910.

Lohfink, Gerhard. 1982. *Jesus and Community: The Social Dimension of Christian Faith.* Trans. John P. Galvin. Philadelphia: Fortress Press.

Luidens, Donald A. 1982. "Bureaucratic Control in a Protestant Denomination." *Journal for the Scientific Study of Religion* 21 (1982):163–175.

Lurkings, E. H. 1975. "Bureaucracy and Moral Order." *The Expository Times* 87 (October):18.

MacIntyre, Alasdair. 1984. *After Virtue: A Study in Moral Theory.* Notre Dame: University of Notre Dame Press. 2nd ed.

——. 1988. *Whose Justice? Which Rationality?* Notre Dame: University of Notre Dame Press.

Marcuse, Herbert, Wolff, Robert Paul, and Moore, Jr., Barrington. 1969. "Repressive Tolerance." In *A Critique of Pure Tolerance.* Boston: Beacon Press. Pp. 81–123. First published 1965.

Marty, Martin E. 1958/1959. *The New Shape of American Religion.* New York: Harper & Brothers.

McConnell, Grant. 1953. *The Decline of Agrarian Democracy.* Berkeley: University of California Press.

McCormick, Richard L. 1981. "The Discovery that Business Corrupts Politics: A Reappraisal of the Origins of Progressivism." *The American Historical Review* 86 (April):259–274.

McGill, Arthur C. 1982. *Suffering: A Test of Theological Method.* Philadelphia: Westminster Press. Orig. publishied 1968.

McKenzie, John L. 1965. *Dictionary of the Bible.* New York: Macmillan, Collier.

McNamara, Robert S. 1995. *In Retrospect: The Tragedy and Lessons of Vietnam.* New York: Random House, Times Books.

Mead, Loren B. 1991. *The Once and Future Church: Reinventing the Congregation for a New Mission Frontier.* Washington, D.C.: Alban Institute.

Mendenhall, George E., and Gary A. Herion. 1992. "Covenant." In *The Anchor Bible Dictionary.* Ed. David Noel Freedman et al. 6 vols. New York: Doubleday & Co.

Messer, Donald E. 1992. *A Conspiracy of Goodness: Contemporary Images of Christian Mission.* Nashville: Abingdon Press.

Mills, Robert. 1976. "Religion and Bureaucracy: A Spiritual Dialogue," *Journal of Religion and Health* 15:295.

Molina, Fernando. 1962. *Existentialism as Philosophy.* Englewood Cliffs: Prentice-Hall.

Moltmann, Jürgen. 1991. *The Crucified God: The Cross of Christ as the Foundation and Criticism of Christian Theology.* Trans. R. A. Wilson and John Bowden. San Francisco: HarperCollins. First published 1974.

Neighbour, Ralph W., Jr. 1990. *Where Do We Go from Here? A Guidebook for Cell Group Churches.* Houston: Touch Publications.

Newbigin, Lesslie. 1989. *The Gospel in a Pluralist Society.* Grand Rapids & Geneva: Eerdmans & WCC Publications.

———. 1994. *A Word in Season: Perspectives on Christian World Missions.* Grand Rapids & Edinburgh: Eerdmans & Saint Andrews Press.

———. 1995. *Proper Confidence: Faith, Doubt, and Certainty in Christian Discipleship.* Grand Rapids: Eerdmans.

Niebuhr, H. Richard. 1935. "The Question of the Church." In Wilhelm Pauck, Francis P. Miller, and H. Richard Niebuhr, *The Church Against the World.* Chicago: Willett, Clark. Pp. 1–13.

———. 1951. *Christ and Culture.* New York: Harper Torchbooks.

Nietzsche, Friedrich. 1901. *The Will to Power.* Trans. Walter Kaufmann. Ed. R. J. Hollingdale. New York: Vintage Books. Repr. 1967 ed.

Palmer, Bruce. 1980. *"Man Over Money": The Southern Populist Critique of American Capitalism.* Chapel Hill: University of North Carolina Press.

Pelling, Henry. 1960. *American Labor.* Chicago: University of Chicago Press.

Pisani, Donald J. 1983. "Reclamation and Social Engineering in the Progressive Era." *Agricultural History* 57 (January):53–58.

Porter, Glenn. 1973. *The Rise of Big Business, 1860–1910.* Arlington Heights: AHM.

Riesman, David, Nathan Glazer, and Reuel Denney. 1953. *The Lonely Crowd: A Study of the Changing American Character.* Garden City: Doubleday Anchor Books. First published. 1950. Abr. ed.

Rodgers, Daniel T. 1978. *The Work Ethic in Industrial America, 1850–1920.* Chicago: University of Chicago Press.

Roof, Wade Clark, and William McKinney. 1987. *American Mainline Religion: Its Changing Shape and Future.* New Brunswick: Rutgers University Press.

Rosato, Philip J. 1983. "Holy Spirit." In *The Westminster Dictionary of Christian Theology.* Ed. Alan Richardson and John Bowden. Philadelphia: Westminster Press.

Schrader, George Alfred, Jr. 1967. "Existential Philosophy: Resurgent Humanism." In *Existential Philosophers: Kierkegaard to Merleau-Ponty.* Ed. Schrader, New York: McGraw-Hill. Pp. 1–44.

Scott, William G., and David K. Hart. 1979. *Organizational America.* Boston: Houghton Mifflin.

Shannon, Fred A. 1945. *The Farmer's Last Frontier: Agriculture, 1860–1897.* New York: Farrar and Rinehart.

Shenk, David W., and Ervin R. Stutzman. 1988. *Creating Communities of the Kingdom: New Testament Models of Church Planting.* Scottdale: Herald Press.

Shinn, Roger L., ed. 1968. *Restless Adventure: Essays on Contemporary Expressions of Existentialism.* New York: Scribner's.

Sklar, Martin J. 1988. *The Corporate Reconstruction of American Capitalism, 1890–1916: The Market, the Law, and Politics*. Cambridge: Cambridge University Press.

Skowronek, Stephen. 1982. *Building a New American State: The Expansion of National Administrative Capacities, 1877–1920*. Cambridge: Cambridge University Press.

Smith, Henry Nash. 1950. *Virgin Land: The American West as Symbol and Myth*. Cambridge: Harvard University Press.

Stivers, Richard. 1994. *The Culture of Cynicism: American Morality in Decline*. Cambridge, Mass.: Blackwell.

Stringfellow, William 1994. "The Constantinian Status Quo." In *A Keeper of the Word: Selected Writings of William Stringfellow*. Ed. and Introd. Bill Wylie Kellerman. Grand Rapids: Eerdmans. Pp. 259–261.

Swan, Martha. 1990. "God Will Not Fail: South Haven United Church of Christ, Bedford, Ohio." In *Good News in Growing Churches*. Ed. Robert L. Burt. New York: Pilgrim Press. Pp. 88–107.

Thompson, E. P. 1978. *The Poverty of Theory and Other Essays*. New York: Monthly Review Press.

Tillich, Paul. 1951. *Reason and Revelation, Being and God*. Vol. 1 of *Systematic Theology*. Chicago: University of Chicago Press.

———. 1952. *The Courage to Be*. New Haven: Yale University Press.

———. 1963. *Life and the Spirit, History and the Kingdom of God*. Vol. 3 of *Systematic Theology*. Chicago: University of Chicago Press.

Tontz, Robert L. 1964. "Memberships of General Farmers' Organizations, United States, 1874–1960." *Agricultural History* 38 (July):145–150.

Tschannen, Oliver. 1994. "Sociological Controversies in Perspective." *Review of Religious Research* 36 (September):70–72.

Ward, James M. 1991. *Thus Says the Lord: The Message of the Prophets*. Nashville: Abingdon Press.

96385

Weber, Max. 1947. *The Theory of Social and Economic Organization.* Trans. A. M. Henderson. Ed. and Intro. Talcott Parsons. Glencoe, Ill.: Free Press & Falcon's Wing Press.

Weeks, Louis. 1991. "The Incorporation of American Religion: The Case of the Presbyterians." *Religion and American Culture* 1 (Winter):112.

Wells, David F. 1993. *No Place for Truth, or Whatever Happened to Evangelical Theology?* Grand Rapids: Eerdmans.

———. 1994. *God in the Wasteland: The Reality of Truth in a World of Fading Dreams.* Grand Rapids: Eerdmans.

White, Jr., Lynn. 1968. *Machina Ex Deo: Essays in the Dynamism of Western Culture.* Cambridge: MIT Press.

Wiebe, Robert H. 1967. *The Search for Order, 1877–1920.* New York: Hill and Wang.

Willard, Dallas. 1988. *The Spirit of the Disciplines: Understanding How God Changes Lives.* San Francisco: HarperCollins.

Willimon, William H. 1990. *Making Disciples: A New Approach to Confirmation.* Inver Grove Heights, Minn.: Logos Productions.

Wink, Walter. 1992. *Engaging the Powers: Discernment and Resistance in a World of Domination.* Minneapolis: Fortress Press.

Wright, Conrad. 1984. "The Growth of Denominational Bureaucracies: A Neglected Aspect of American Church History." *Harvard Theological Review* 77 (1984):178–179.

Wuthnow, Robert. 1988. *The Restructuring of American Religion: Society and Faith Since World War II.* Princeton: Princeton University Press.

Wyllie, Irvin G. 1954. *The Self-Made Man in America: The Myth of Rags to Riches.* New Brunswick: Rutgers University Press.

Zinn, Howard. 1980. *A People's History of the United States.* New York: Harper Colophon.